T5-CCU-808

TAKING A YEAR OFF FROM WORK

LES ABROMOVITZ

J. FLORES
PUBLICATIONS
P.O. BOX 830131
MIAMI, FL 33283-0131

TAKING A YEAR OFF FROM WORK by Les Abromovitz

Copyright © 1994 by Les Abromovitz

Published by:
J. Flores Publications
P.O. Box 830131
Miami, FL 33283-0131

Direct inquires and/or order to the above address.

ISBN 0-918751-15-2

Library of Congress Catalog Card Number: 94-71398

Printed in the United States of America

Nobody ever laid on their deathbed, wishing they'd spent more time at work.

Phil, the restaurant owner
Murphy Brown

CONTENTS

INTRODUCTION

While riding the airport bus late one night, a well-dressed woman in her forties spoke with a stranger in the seat next to her. "There are so many things I want to do with my life, so I'm retiring in seven years."

Perhaps, talking about early retirement helps get you through a long day on the road as you wait in rental car lines, sit on the runway, or watch television in a lonely hotel room. When you're not fighting the traffic to the airport, you're spending hours commuting to and from your job.

Waiting seven years or longer is no easy trick when the flight attendant is serving the Italian combo, the same meal you've eaten on your eleven other flights this month. It's an impossible task when you're listening again to the rental car agent try to sell you the collision damage waiver for yet another vehicle and you can't even remember what your own car looks like.

If you're years away from the age when you can retire, you might be afraid of facing a situation you've seen all too often. Within months after retiring, a friend or co-worker goes under the knife for open heart surgery or dies before really enjoying his retirement. Events like these can make you impatient for the day you can retire. Tragedies like these might make you inclined to take a break from work, while you're young and healthy enough to enjoy it.

Maybe, it hasn't been a tragic event that has caused you to think about a time in your life when you're not working. You may be feeling that each day is exactly the same as the day before. Going to work each day and doing the same job can make you question the value of what you do and what life's all about. You might be headed for a mid-life crisis, triggered by this nine-to-five routine.

Or maybe you've reached the point where you can barely drag yourself in to work each day. It's not that you've just grown tired of the same old job. You've learned to hate it. When you wake up in the morning, you no longer greet the day with anticipation. Instead, you're in a bad mood again because your time and talent is being wasted in your current position.

Worse yet, your mood doesn't improve after your morning coffee. You sit through meeting after meeting, thinking about how many better things you could be doing with your time. At the end of the day, your major accomplishment is reducing the pile of paper on your desk and shuffling it off to someone else who probably feels as frustrated as you do.

If you find yourself in any of these situations, you may feel your options are limited. One solution is to tell yourself that you have a vacation coming up next month. When the two weeks come and go, however, you're back in the same situation from which you tried to escape. Worse yet, no one's touched your desk for two weeks and you'll need to work even longer hours than normal, just to keep your head above water.

Two weeks off just doesn't do the trick when you feel the need to do something different with your life and you can't swing early retirement. The stress and frustration continue to build, because there are so many dreams you want to pursue. A voice inside urges you to chuck it all, but you still have responsibilities and assets you want to protect.

Your benefits statement from work looks great, as long as you stay with the company until the year 2017. If you last that long, you'll live quite well in retirement. Perhaps, you're not that optimistic about how well you'll fare in retirement. Many baby boomers are extremely skeptical about Social Security and have minimal expectations about receiving benefits from the system. These baby boomers see the normal retirement age going beyond the traditional 65 years of age.

You've been in the work force for years without a break and are missing out on the little things that make life worthwhile. You're frazzled by the day-after-day grind caused by your job. Because of career demands, you've never been able to try a different life style. You want to travel, write a book, refinish furniture, study music or pursue a dozen other interests that you've had for years.

Perhaps, you have less cerebral endeavors in mind. You might simply want to walk the beach, look at the sunset, fish, improve your tennis game, golf, play volleyball, go to the movies, or just walk around the neighborhood every morning instead of rushing for the bus and gulping down your breakfast.

You probably don't have time for hobbies, whether it be stamp collecting or working with stained glass. You might be a Civil War buff who wants to read and learn about that era. Maybe you're like one lawyer who crafts miniature doll houses and even decorates each room with wallpaper and wood floors. This former judge attends classes in Maine to further refine his craft.

Your own special interests may take you to Maine, Europe, or no farther than your den. Wherever the locale, it's doubtful you have enough time to work on them now. Until you spend more time with those hobbies, you'll never really know if you'd enjoy working full-time on those projects or if you'd like to operate a business that incorporates your favorite pastime.

Strange as it seems, you might even want to take a year off to work, but at something you can really love. Maybe you'd like to land a job near the ocean or in a resort community. It wouldn't matter that the job pays far less than you make now, because it's your year off. You might find the lower pay doesn't matter, as long as you're in a warmer climate or aren't as stressed out as you are now.

Two weeks is never enough but a year will be. Try to imagine it ...a year off to do everything you've always wanted. It's the next best thing to your dream of early retirement and, certainly, a great deal more realistic.

I wish I could counsel you on how to retire early. There are dozens of books on that subject and they may have the solution. Retirement may not, however, be the end-all that you think it is.

You're probably skeptical, as you should be. You're thinking, "Oh sure, I'll just walk in tomorrow and ask for the year off. The boss will throw me out on my ear." You're right. It's much more difficult than that and it will take a great deal of planning. But it can be done.

Don't underestimate how much planning you must do. There will be many legal, financial, tax, pension, and health insurance issues to consider. If you plan on traveling or living elsewhere during your year off, you still need to take care of your present home while you're away. And since you probably will still need to work for a living after you return, your plan should safeguard your ability to find a job waiting for you when your year off is completed.

Most employers do not provide for a sabbatical. Colleges and universities offer sabbaticals after a prescribed period of time. Many people say that the academic environment is not the real world and in this case it's true. In the business world, most employers won't permit their employees to take a sabbatical.

The year off, nonetheless, can be the solution to your current dilemma. You're burned out and sick of the career path you've chosen. Or you might even love your job, but the demands of your career infringe greatly upon your personal life. Unless you're a one-dimensional human being or a workaholic, there's more that you want to do with your life.

There's no guarantee your employer will permit it or that it won't cause financial problems. Taking a year off isn't as attractive as early retirement but it can help you dig out of the rut you're in now. Although you may need to hold a job for the indefinite future, you can work out a year off if you really want to.

As you plan for that year off, you may learn a lot about yourself. You might find that work is not the source of your dissatisfaction and time off isn't the answer. It could be that you need a new career, not a year off from your current job. If nothing else, planning for your year off can give you a new perspective on your career and your life.

Not everyone will be able to swing a year off right away. It may take an extended period of financial planning and more discipline than some readers can muster. Others will find they don't have the right temperament to take a year off.

For those who are willing to work hard and plan extensively, a year off is not an unrealistic goal. The strategy is not risk-free but it's far less dangerous than giving up everything you've worked so hard to achieve. You will be taking drastic action to change your life for a year or perhaps longer.

In the sixties, it used to be fashionable for college students to take a year off to find themselves. Perhaps, you never had that luxury. You may have been involved with more pressing issues like raising a family, the draft, earning a living, working to pay your tuition, or other less fashionable activities. Years later, you find yourself in a career that you chose, but didn't really choose. For a host of reasons, you stuck with it even though it's far less enjoyable than it once was, and it may not have been much fun to begin with.

This book isn't about making a career change, although it may be one of the many avenues you want to explore during your year off. It's about making time to think and to look introspectively. It's about creating other options, based upon your interests. It's about expanding your activities outside of work, so that you can move in a new direction or return to your current job with a renewed sense of purpose. It's about taking a year off from work.

Taking a year off may mean giving up some things. But it may also mean giving up some other things like airport buses, airline food, sitting on the runway, long lines at rental car counters, lonely hotel rooms, hours of commuting time, endless meetings, and mornings when you'd rather do anything but go to work. For at least a year, you can choose how you want to spend each and every day.

FROM THE FAST LANE TO THE CHECK-OUT LINE

You walk into the boss' office. "Boss, I'll be blunt," you say. "I never get to see my kids. I don't have time to pursue any of my outside interests. I'm on the road three weeks a month. I never get home before seven in the evening. In short, I make a good buck but the quality of my life leaves a lot to be desired, so I want to take a year off."

"Gee," the boss says as she hangs her head in shame. "I never knew we were pushing you this hard. Because you're one of our most valued employees, I want you to take that year off ...with full pay."

As long as you're dreaming, enjoy it. Maybe, the boss will let you keep the company car for the year too. Unfortunately, this scenario is a fantasy, unless one of your parents happens to own the company you work for or is chairman of the board. Even then, you'll probably find it difficult to take a year off, let alone getting paid while you're gone.

For this reason, we'll start with the assumption that you won't be getting paid during your year off. If you can negotiate a more profitable arrangement with your employer such as those we'll discuss in subsequent chapters, all the better. Nevertheless, there's a lot more to taking a year off than just money.

WHOSE LIFE IS IT ANYWAY?

Taking a year off makes a statement about your values. It says that having time for yourself is a higher priority than making money. But, if owning a new Jaguar is more important to you than doing what you want with your time for a year, you're not ready yet. You may never be ready.

For some, their desire to take a year off may be the result of family values. Perhaps, they've become strangers to their spouse and children because of work obligations. A year off can give them the time to cement those family bonds again.

Taking a year off has a lot to do with dreams but not necessarily the dream of being rich. In fact, a sabbatical from work may postpone the day when you are independently wealthy. It can, however, keep you from postponing the time when you'll finally get around to making those dreams a reality. As you approach midlife and realize you're not getting any younger, it's time to make your move. Nevertheless, the year off should not be allowed to destroy the financial security you've worked so hard to achieve.

Perhaps, you already have a plan for taking a year off. Every day, you buy a fistful of lottery tickets and pray. Or maybe you're waiting for your rich aunt to die and make it possible for you to take a year off.

Assuming you're routinely getting only one number

out of six on your lottery card and your aunt is taking lambada lessons, a more proactive strategy might be just the ticket. Obviously, you have dozens of questions about how to take a year off. Initially, however, you have to ask yourself a number of questions. The first is what you intend to do with your year off.

Maybe you want to sit around the house, looking like Ed Norton in *The Honeymooners*. Perhaps, you'd like to wake up in the morning and not have to shave or put on your make-up. You might like to fix breakfast for your children instead of racing to the day care center.

It's not enough to know in general terms what you want to do with your year off. We'd all like to search for the meaning of life but that's not enough justification for taking a year-long break. You have to be more specific.

Start writing down exactly what you want to do during your sabbatical. Make sure these pursuits really require a year off and aren't just one-shot activities that you could do now, but just haven't gotten around to it. You may want to go parasailing in Acapulco or take up skydiving, but you don't need a year off to do it.

As you outline your schedule of activities, be certain your wish list isn't filled with activities that will strain the tight budget you'll be on during your year off. If you want to make it on Broadway and live in New York City during your year off, the higher cost of living is going to be a challenge. Although there are ways to cope with these additional expenses, taking a year off will be more diffi-cult under those circumstances.

After you've worked on your list, allow yourself a cooling off period. Put the list away for a few weeks and then see if the activities are just as appealing as they were when you wrote them down. Make certain that your lack of time isn't just an excuse and that there isn't some other reason why you haven't engaged in the activity ...like fear.

Knowing what you want to do during your year off is also important, because it has a direct impact on the planning process. In later chapters, we'll discuss specific issues you'll face if you plan on traveling or living elsewhere during your year off. Your home can be an important source of funds for your year off. Therefore, it is important to decide immediately where you intend to spend your time away from work.

There are a few restrictions on what you can do during your year off. You can't go to the mall every day during your year off, especially if you're a shopaholic. Worse yet, your purchasing power is going to diminish significantly during this time away from work. Now, if you want to go to the mall every day to walk for exercise and won't be tempted to shop afterwards, you're moving in the right direction.

TIME OFF FOR GOOD BEHAVIOR

There's a lot to be learned from taking this year off, information that can educate you on how you want to spend your next decades in the work force. If you plan to try out a different career or life-style during your year off, it can lead to self-awareness and teach you more about your dreams than you care to know. The year off can show you that dreams aren't always what they're cracked up to be and a few new ones are in order.

Perhaps, you've dreamed of getting out from behind that desk and working in the outdoors. Maybe you'd like to try your hand at being a white water rafting guide. Unfortunately, you may find that working in the outdoors isn't as glamorous as it appears from your office. It's a little like camping. It might be fun for a few weeks each year, but living in the wilderness may not be as pleasing as a regular life-style.

You may find that even your hobbies aren't as much fun as full-time endeavors. If you plan on pursuing a business that incorporates your hobby, you may learn that it's not worth the time and effort you're investing in it. You could find that when you try to earn money from your hobby, it's a job and not nearly as enjoyable as it once was.

The problem when you open any business, even one that involves a hobby you love, is that it requires many activities that aren't fun. You'll be bogged down in more mundane matters such as bookkeeping, accounting, taxes, marketing, and inventory management.

You may have dozens of interests, but you need to have a clear understanding of how you want to spend your day. Excuses like, "I don't even have time to think about that until I'm done working," won't cut it. You'll need to do a considerable amount of thinking and planning before you take the drastic step of arranging a year off. If you can't pinpoint what you intend to do during this year off, it's time to regroup.

Despite that admonition, it is quite clear that almost everyone who works for a living needs more time. After you're done investing all of your energy in your job, there's very little time left for your family and your interests. Because of the constraints placed upon you by your career, you barely have a moment for yourself. With a little planning though, you can have a year's worth of moments when you're not exhausted from the pressures of work.

You might want to write the Great American Novel during your year off. While that is certainly a fine ambition, you need to anticipate the setbacks you might experience. Are you going to be sorry you took a year off if you experience writers' block or find rejection letters in your mail each day? If you don't like what you're doing during this year off or find it's not everything you dreamed of, you're headed for disappointment.

Chances are, you don't want to take a year off to do nothing. Although you've achieved a lot over the years, there's still a dream that you want to pursue. It may not come true during your year off, but it's time to give it a shot.

You need to ask yourself why you want a year off. "That's an easy one," you're thinking. "I hate my job and my boss is a jerk." Although that might be true, the solution to your problem is more likely a new job rather than a year off. A year off isn't necessarily the answer to a career situation that you hate. You should be exploring other options, along with the year off. Besides, if your boss is as big a jerk as you say, you won't find a sympathetic ear when you ask for time off.

You must distinguish between needing a change of scenery and needing a year off. Maybe you're just sick of the people you work with and are bored with your present job duties. As you prepare for your year off, you can explore other employment options that might remedy this problem. In the end, you may decide you don't need a year off.

Maybe, you need a year off, just so you can slow down. The pace of your life is causing you physical problems. You might be a candidate for heart disease, because of the high-pressured life you lead. Of course, if you're a Type A personality, you'll probably find a way to drive yourself even when you have a year off.

As you analyze why you need time off, you could find that something less than one year will do. You may want to live or work in a resort community that only operates on a seasonal basis. Your dream might be to take a world cruise and be gone only three months.

Maybe what you're looking for is freedom ...freedom from bosses, red tape, nine to five, rules and regulations. You want more flexible hours and independence. It's the same reasons many people want to open a business of their own. Maybe you're just looking for freedom from responsibility for a year.

What you're undoubtably looking for is more balance in your life ...a year of more play and less work. For many, taking a year off will help them get their priorities in order. It will mean that you can spend more time with your family, even if certain financial goals have to be placed on the back burner.

No matter why you want a year off, the benefits can be enormous. It can recharge your batteries, batteries that have been drained over years in the work force. The year off for most people can reduce stress for the next twelve months and lead to a life-style where stress is manageable.

You still need to answer the question of when should you take this year off. Sorry, tomorrow is out of the question. Once you're certain that this year off is the route to take, there will be weeks and months of planning ahead of you before you can take the plunge.

It could be even longer for some readers. If you've just gotten into a new home or have two children in college, now is not a good time to take your year off even though the kids might qualify for more financial aid.

The implementation of your plan may be delayed if you're not in control of your finances. You may be having problems now, despite the fact that you earn a good living. If you're worried about how you'll handle a year off without pay, you should be. You need to get your finances in order and move toward taking a year off from there. Fortunately, if you follow the steps outlined in this book, you can help yourself get out of debt while pushing closer to the time when you can take a year off.

Finally, you must answer the key question for our purposes which is how to arrange this year off, financially and logistically.

THE PSYCHOLOGY OF TAKING A YEAR OFF

A greeting card gives this message: "You're retiring? You know what that means—Now when someone says, 'Have a nice day,' you might actually have a shot at it."

When someone tells you to have a nice day now, you probably glare at him. First of all, you're sick of strangers telling you to have a nice day. More importantly, if it's a work day, you may have reached the point where there isn't a chance in hell that you'll have a nice day.

Hopefully, during your year off, you'll look forward to every morning, something you aren't doing now. Even if you come back to the same job, the year off can provide a new perspective on work and your career. Regardless of what happens down the road, you'll have a shot a hundreds of nice days if you take a year off.

In some respects, you'll be in the same boat as retirees. You can expect to face many of the same psychological issues that retirees encounter, even though you'll be rejoining the work force in a year. Retirees often have difficulty adjusting to life after work. Their identity is defined by their jobs and they lose sight of who they are and the contribution they make to society.

Nahhh. You won't have that problem. If your life was your work, you'd hardly be thinking about taking a year off. Don't be so sure.

Though you may resist the notion, you probably derive a certain amount of self-esteem from your work. Try to anticipate some of the situations you'll find yourself in during your year off. Suppose you go to a class reunion. Are you going to brag about how you're taking a year off or will you tell them about that wonderful career you'll be resuming in twelve months? Are you going to worry they won't believe it was a voluntary act on your part? Will they think you were let go and dreamed up this face-saving maneuver?

Of course, the ideal solution is to take a copy of this book to your reunion so they'll know it was your decision. In all seriousness, however, you must consider the reaction you'll get from family and friends to your decision. Unless you're absolutely comfortable with that decision, you might find yourself in an awkward situation when it's time to explain what you do for a living.

If you're like a lot of people, you go to the shore for your vacation. As your vacation comes to an end and you think about returning to work, jobs at the beach become particularly inviting. You're ready to hand out tickets for winning scores in skeeball or to sell pork rolls on the Boardwalk. Maybe you want to work in a bait shop or work on the water.

Who knows? Maybe you'd grow tired of that life-style after a few months. Perhaps, it can be aggravating running a game where vacationers try to catapult a rubber frog onto a floating lilly pad in the hope of winning valuable prizes, prizes that you stick onto the windows of your car with the suction cups on their feet. You might soon find out that you have more hassles in that line of work than you normally do. After awhile, you might become disillusioned with the prospects of a life where you hand out six-foot stuffed giraffes to people who have no use for them.

Worse yet, what if you run into friends from the City when you're working at some menial job, albeit in the climate of your dreams? Will you feel the need to explain that you're on hiatus from work and that you're simply revitalizing yourself with a break from your chosen profession? On the other hand, seeing you in that setting may strike a chord with your friends who may always have dreamed of getting away from it all.

My wife and I have gone to the Jersey shore for many years. We always visit a wonderfully tacky beach community and invariably hate to leave. We ran into a Philadelphia lawyer who rented bikes during the Summer season. We weren't quite sure if he returned to the practice of law during the Winter. Each time we drove past his stand on our way home, there was no question that we would have traded places with him.

RISK TOLERANCE

The psychological considerations associated with taking a year off are similar to the psychology of investing. You have to take a look at your risk tolerance. This is a subjective analysis and will be different for every reader.

You must be comfortable with the risks you'll be taking if you follow through on this plan.

Just as you'll find with investments, certain people are more comfortable with risk than others. Looking at your investment portfolio should give you a clear picture of the risks you're willing to take. If you've always shied away from the stock market so you can stick with an insured savings account, the odds are good you have little tolerance for risk. It may also be an indication that you won't be able to handle the risks incumbent with taking a year off from work.

Don't close the book quite yet. We will also discuss less extreme solutions that more cautious readers can utilize to get a break from work. We'll discuss financial strategies that should appeal to those with little tolerance for risk.

For some, the concept of taking a year off from work will be a tremendous blow to their sense of security. The employee who has worked for the same employer for twenty years and hates the thought of change will suffer tremendous psychological upheaval when exploring the year off option. Those who fall in this category will resist change, even when their job has grown wearisome, aggravating and boring. The person who has changed jobs frequently is less likely to be frightened by the prospect of cutting ties with his employer.

Comparing your investment temperament isn't the conclusive test for determining whether you're a candidate for a year off. Just because you feel better with conservative investments like certificates of deposit or savings bonds doesn't mean you'll never work up the courage to take a year off. There are both conservative and risky approaches to this goal. Obviously, someone with little risk tolerance will gravitate toward the more conservative strategy. Nevertheless, it very well may be that those who shun risks will adapt well to a methodical and disciplined plan to take a year off.

No matter how thoroughly you plan, there are some unavoidable risks involved with taking a year off. Here are just a few:

- You may lose some of the possessions you've worked so hard to accumulate.
- Your career may be set back enormously.
- Your long-term career prospects and salary may suffer indefinitely because of this year off.
- You'll find it hard to find a job after your year off.
- You'll find your year off is more stressful than working.

You have to go into your year off knowing that you may not have a job to come back to. But if you're working on another proposal until three in the morning or must spend your weekend preparing an appellate brief, it may not matter. In some ways, taking a year off can extend your career and your life. You may be ready to give your notice today and this option can help you avoid making a terrible mistake.

CURTAILING THOSE RISKS

You may not realize that it's sometimes more risky to do nothing than to take decisive action. Let's suppose you own a house in a deteriorating neighborhood and you're afraid to take a chance on moving up to a nicer home. Because of your indecisiveness, you stay where you are and your investment becomes virtually worthless.

Your work environment might also be deteriorating. If you're afraid of change, you may be going down with a sinking ship. In actuality, you could have very little to lose by taking a year off.

Whether your career is on the up-swing or going down the toilet, there are ways to control those risks. One of the ways to insure that you'll hate your year off is by giving up everything you've worked so hard to achieve. This year off cannot be anything but disappointing if you lose your career and your life savings as a result.

It might help to make a comparison to gambling. When you go into a casino, many experts suggest setting a limit on how much you can afford to lose. Going beyond that limit is a way to guarantee disaster. Similarly, only a portion of your funds should be utilized for taking a year off from work. If you do give up everything to take a year off, it can never live up to your expectations.

In some respects, it's like going to a restaurant that costs $50 per meal versus one that charges $10 for each dinner. Your expectations with the $50 meal are greater. In a similar vein, when you pay $100 for a bottle of wine as opposed to the $5 variety with a screw cap, you often set yourself up for disappointment. In any event, if you plan on taking a year off, there will be few $50 dinners and $100 bottles of wine in your future. In fact, you might even have to give up the $10 dinner out.

Something in your own upbringing might make you

unwilling to deprive yourself. It isn't as easy to jump off the fast track as you might think. Still, *Time* Magazine reported on April 8, 1991, that Americans are embracing simpler pleasures in place of materialism. Sales of BMW's are down, while Honda sales are up. While there may be a trend in that direction, it doesn't necessarily mean you're willing to make the kinds of sacrifices necessary to take a year off.

Preparing for your year off will certainly test your ability to delay gratification. Although your year off is months away, you'll be paying for it with today's sacrifices. You may find it especially hard to pass up immediate gratification so that the dream of a year off can become a reality. Nonetheless, if you spent years saving for college, a new home, or a new car, you've already demonstrated the maturity and discipline necessary to prepare for a year off.

On the positive side, while you may be delaying gratification, it could be a whole lot worse. You could be dangling the carrot of retirement to motivate yourself. Knowing that you can retire in twenty years is a tough way to get yourself through the day. The goal of taking a year off is within the reach of most readers.

To be psychologically ready for your year off, you have to make certain it is a higher priority than the luxuries you've come to enjoy. You can start by making a list of what you're willing to give up and what you won't give up under any circumstances. Make sure you consistently feel the same way about your priority list and that your attitudes don't change after an especially frantic week at work.

If you're married, it's not just your own attitudes that you must consider. Suppose your spouse plans to continue working and doesn't wish to take a year off. Although that employment may brighten your financial picture, It can also lead to discord between you. Your spouse will feel the impact of the family austerity program and may be bothered by it. Many spouses won't be able to cope with cutting back, while not sharing in the benefits of the year off.

When you are the spouse taking the year off, you must be cognizant of this very natural reaction. Depending upon how you're spending your year off, you can neutralize that resentment by taking on additional responsibilities at home that your spouse usually handles. The spouse taking the year off should also be prepared to make most of the financial sacrifices.

Your husband or wife will find there is a positive side to your taking a year off. Maybe, the family can have a dinner conversation where you don't complain about work. You might prove to be a much more charming spouse when not stressed-out by work. Ideally, however, a married couple will take a year off together to pursue a dream they share because of compatible interests. It's tougher to swing financially but will be worth the effort.

You must be comfortable with the trade-offs you are making. Most readers aren't, nor should they be, willing to trade all of their worldly possessions for a year off. It wouldn't take long to regret your decision.

You won't be able to sustain the life-style you're used to living. On the other hand, you shouldn't be forced to give up your long-term life-style. If you own a home, having a year off isn't worth losing it. Buying that house was probably a dream come true for you and it's important in maintaining your sense of security and well-being. Besides, moving back in with Mom and Dad is not likely a trade-off you're willing to make for a year off.

MIND GAMES

If you're not prepared financially for your hiatus from the work force, your year off will be a stressful one. There is an obvious correlation between financial problems and stress. You must be confident that you can survive financially during your year off and should make allowances for the mini-traumas that will invariably happen in the course of your year off. The car will go on the fritz or the washer will go to appliance heaven. Unless you plan carefully for those problems, your spirits will fall in the dumper when those events occur.

You can expect a dose of depression at various points during your year off. Hopefully, if all goes well, this won't occur until it's time for you to reenter the work force. We will deal with this inevitable depression at length in Chapter 15. The stress caused by financial problems, however, is avoidable in many instances.

When you're pulling the reigns in financially and counting pennies, money will become a financial issue in your mind. It will help to anticipate what can go wrong. By doing so, you can avoid the stress associated with those problems.

If the car you drive is being held together by chewing gum and spit, you shouldn't be surprised if it craps out during your year off. Before you begin your year off, make a list of what is likely to go wrong that will throw a monkey wrench in your budget. Although you can't avoid grinding your teeth when these events occur, you'll be in a better frame of mind than you would be otherwise.

There are going to be times when the psychology involved with taking a year off and sound financial advice won't mesh. Your peace of mind is a more important priority than making the smartest financial move. You should be stocking up on high-priced items before your year off, even though sound inventory management suggests that you buy them as you need them. The just-in-time inventory system may be the most efficient use of your resources, but it won't help your disposition when you're drawing large amounts from your savings.

You should be stocking up on the necessities now instead of later. If there's a great sale, buy much of what you'll need for your year off, whether that be shoes, typewriter ribbons, or toilet paper. Buy a case of tennis balls instead of feeling guilty each time you play during your year off. You might even end up saving money by buying these products in bulk and by cheating inflation. More importantly, you don't want to be out there buying things when your mind tells you that saving money is a priority.

Remember now that you can't use this logic as an excuse to go out on a shopping spree. You can't say, "I'll need this item during my year off, so I'd better buy it now." We're restricting our discussion here to the purchase of necessities or products that you'll need for the activities planned during your year off. If your idea of a wonderful year off is wearing a new outfit each day, you're going to have problems. It will be almost impossible to fulfill your psychological needs within the financial parameters we'll discuss in Chapter 3.

You can also reduce financial stress by paying some bills in advance, when feasible. Perhaps, your cable company offers a discount for paying bills a year in advance. Pay your car insurance bill in full instead of on the installment plan. You'll pay less and it will be one less bill that bothers you each month. While you're at it, notify your car insurer if you'll be driving less during your year off which will reduce your premium further.

It will also help psychologically to keep separate bank accounts, a topic we will discuss more in Chapter 3. Although you might earn more interest by keeping your funds in one place, your state of mind is more important. It also might help if you don't feel you're losing too much money by taking a year off. If you can earn extra money now in some fashion, you'll feel less guilty during your year off. Of course, if you're stressed out now, the last thing you need is to work harder, even though it's in anticipation of taking a year off.

In Chapter 3, we will also discuss how to budget for your year off so that you won't have to worry about money for awhile. Unfortunately, if you worry about money now, taking a year off won't put your mind at ease. You may become preoccupied with this subject when your cash flow is curtailed.

The shift in your cash flow can be disconcerting, no matter how well you plan. When you're working, your cash is replenished as you spend it. You're putting away money in a 401k plan most likely and your employer is matching those savings up to a particular percentage. When you take a year off from work, you're draining those resources rather than watching them grow. Obviously, you have to deal with the mind set that you should be in the saving mode rather than watching your assets diminish.

If you were retiring at the usual age rather than just taking a year off, this problem wouldn't be so burdensome. You would be drawing a pension or receiving a Social Security check. The cash flow problem wouldn't be so difficult psychologically to deal with in that instance. Of course, there are many older people who never seem to realize that they can shift from a saving to a spending mode.

You, on the other hand, may never have been much of a saver. The idea of living on a budget bothers you. Many baby boomers who make a good buck still find it difficult to save. If you intend to take a year off, you have to be mentally prepared to live within a tight budget.

SELF ASSESSMENT

You have to overcome your fears. The idea of taking a year off can scare your socks off, if you really think about it. My intent is not to talk you into taking a year off. Rather, I am simply trying to show that it is possible, if you're willing to make sacrifices. You may be carrying too much psychological baggage for it to be a viable option. There will be some whose temperament will never allow them to enjoy or benefit from this year off.

You shouldn't need therapy to uncover some of the personality quirks that stand in the way of your taking a year off. If security is important to you, the uncertainties of taking a year off can overwhelm the positive aspects you'll derive from taking this time for yourself.

It might help for you to take an informal psychological quiz. There are no right or wrong answers and no points given for a particular response. Taking this quiz won't tell you if you're an ideal candidate for a year off but it can open your eyes to many of the issues you'll face. Ask yourself:

- How materialistic am I?
- Will money issues interfere with my enjoyment?
- Can I function without the structure of work?
- Will I be bored during my year off?
- Will I eat out of boredom or become depressed?
- Am I comfortable with the risks of a year off?
- Do I like my job? Will I miss the people?
- How will I feel if a competitor gets a promotion I've wanted while I'm out?
- Does my work give me a sense of pride?
- If I won the lottery, would I keep working?
- If I have to work for a living, what's my dream job?
- Have I been out of work before and how was it?
- Will my family be supportive of my decision?
- What are my career goals?
- What are my financial goals?

As you make plans for your year off, you'll learn more about yourself and how you want to spend the rest of your life.

SUMMARY

Maybe, you're ready to give up now. If so, you can use the ultimate psychological tool which is to rationalize why it can't be done. It's a lot easier and certainly requires a lot less discipline than developing a plan to take a year off. As you climb on the bus each morning at 6:00, you can tell yourself that it can't be done and that you're better off working for the next twenty years.

FINANCIAL GROUNDWORK

It's 4:30 in the morning and you're wide awake. Because of aggravation from work, you've been having trouble getting a good night's sleep.

Instead of tossing and turning, you go downstairs to watch television. Of course, it's not really television you're watching. The only thing you can find to watch is infomercials for every imaginable product.

For awhile, you watch people grind carrots into juice. Then you listen to testimonials for $150 sunglasses. From there, you switch to an infomercial with Fran Tarkenton selling motivational tapes. On a different channel, he's involved in another lengthy advertisement, only this time Tarkenton is selling an entrepreneurial course. The pitch goes something like this:

"Are you stuck in a dead-end job, surrounded by incompetents who are going to the top?" he asks.

"No, I'm perfectly satisfied with my career," you reply to the screen. "That's why I'm up at 4:30 in the morning watching you. And if you weren't on, I'd be watching Erin Gray talking about make-up in the wee hours of the morning."

In the hope of finding a horror film to watch, you

switch channels. Instead of a horror film, you find John Davidson in Hawaii, promoting a real estate investment course that will make you financially independent. You press the remote control again and find another real estate course that's going to make you rich. The course, consisting of tapes and books, guarantees that you'll be able to retire in two years or less.

Even though the infomercials claim that real estate investment is the answer, it's the mortgage on one piece of property that's holding you back. When your end-of-the-year statement arrives, you find you've barely made a dent in the principal of the mortgage on your house. The monthly payment, along with the real estate taxes, are a few of the major obligations that keep you from retiring early, or even taking a year off.

Although your home has probably been your best investment, it's unlikely that you want to buy any more real estate. Furthermore, most readers won't want to sell their present home, even though they've made a great deal of money on paper. Otherwise, financing a year away from work wouldn't be that difficult. If you're a reader who wants to buy and sell real estate to achieve financial independence, you'd better switch one of those infomercials back on.

If keeping your home isn't an issue, you can do what Albert Brooks did in the movie, Lost in America. The Brooks character persuaded his wife to drop out of society with him. They liquidated their assets, bought a mobile home, and set off across America.

The key to taking a year off is totally different. What you really need is a financial plan that won't leave you homeless when your year off is finished. Although you can expect to drain some of your resources during the year off, you don't want to lose those assets that you've worked so hard to accumulate.

With this in mind, you have to ask yourself some difficult financial questions. Here are just a few:

- Do you have the discipline to live within a tight budget?
- Are you prepared to give up luxury items like eating out or expensive clothes?
- Are you satisfied with the house you're in or do you hope to trade up in the next few years?
- Will you be up at 4:30 in the morning, worrying about money instead of being aggravated over by your job?
- Will you cut corners with your family's safety if money is tight? Will you drive on bald tires or skip health exams because of the cost?
- Will you take financial shortcuts instead of methodically planning for a year off?

As you ask yourself these and other questions, remember that you can't use a year off to run away from your financial and family obligations.

There are two issues here. Do you want to take a year off? And if you decide it's a dream you want to pursue, ask yourself:

Can I afford to take a year off? Even if you can scrape together the cash necessary to take a year off, can you afford to give up a year's pay, along with the perks that most people depend upon to solidify their financial future? You're not just losing your salary, but a whole lot more.

It's a year where you're not contributing to your retirement savings plan. Right now, you're probably putting away a certain percentage of your salary before taxes. Your employer adds a sizable amount to your contribution. The entire amount grows in a tax-deferred account until you're ready to retire.

In addition, it's possible you'll do damage to your pension by taking a year off. This is an especially dangerous possibility if you plan to retire in the next few years.

You may not be able to give up your benefits for a year either. There's health, life, and disability insurance to consider. You may be one of the many whose total insurance package is tied to your job. Regardless of whether you take a year off or not, that's a problem. Nevertheless, these insurance issues will be addressed in Chapter 12.

Therefore, it's obvious you're not just losing your salary for the year or longer if your employer won't guarantee you a job upon your return. You're also losing your benefits which usually equate to about a third of your salary.

Before you take the next step, you have to look at whether you're on solid footing now. Look first at your emergency fund. Financial planning experts recommend that you have three to six months in ready cash available in case of emergencies. If you don't have that minimum amount saved, you're not ready yet to implement a financial strategy that will lead to your year off.

Grab hold of your belt. Taking a year off is going to

involve a lot of belt-tightening. It's going to be a year where you live within a tight budget. You're in for problems if you budget like some people do. They take out enough cash to last until the next payday, but then hit the banking machine twice when they run short.

Living within a budget can be especially trying if you plan on traveling during your year off. Most people view vacations as a time to splurge and be freer with their money. They'll spend far more on a given day than they would at home, and that's not just for a hotel. Many indulge themselves with expensive purchases. While you're planning for a 52 week vacation from work, you're not on a 52 week vacation where money can be frittered away. Even if you're traveling in the South of France, you have to stay on a budget. Unfortunately, the Moulin Rouge or the Carleton in Cannes won't necessarily fall within those parameters.

If you're going to stick close to home, there will be savings from not working. You'll eliminate lunches out, business clothes, and dry cleaning costs. Assuming you haven't won an office pool yet, you'll cut out those dozens of minor expenditures at the office that nibble away at your paycheck.

Most readers will save a bundle on commuting costs during their year off. If you drive to work, you can even notify your car insurer that your mileage is reduced. This might save you a few dollars on your premium.

You'll also save on taxes. As we'll discuss in Chapter 13, the timing of your year off can make a big difference in your tax bill.

It's not a hopeless situation. The July 1, 1992 edition

of the *Wall Street Journal* talked about a woman who managed to save $70,000 to start a magazine. She achieved this goal by moonlighting, investing, and living cheaply.

With the goal of taking a year off in mind, you have to plan your own route to get there. At a minimum, you must cut expenses and save more. And you must find a way to generate income during your year off or live off your assets.

TIGHTENING YOUR BELT A NOTCH OR SIX

Like it or not, you need to go on an austerity program now. You can't just make plans to cut your expenses, once your year off has begun. It's important to test the water now, before you take the plunge into your year off. You need to know if you can deal with the budget restrictions necessary for your time off. Otherwise, you'll be in over your head as you go deeper into the execution of your plan.

Obviously, you'll be cutting your expenses over many months before you take a year off. As you exercise self-discipline and take control of your finances, you'll learn if you have the character to handle this lifestyle for the long-term.

Maybe your problem will be just the opposite. If you've always been a good saver, you may have difficulty adjusting to not putting away money. Worse yet, you'll be depleting your existing savings, not putting away money.

Unfortunately, when you're saving for your year away from work, it won't be easy to save for other goals like your child's college education or retirement. That doesn't mean, however, that you should pass up free money so you can build your year off fund. If your employer matches all or part of your contribution to a retirement savings plan, it doesn't make sense to give up this benefit. Dropping out of the 401(k) retirement savings plan that your employer offers will also increase the amount you pay out in taxes.

It would not be wise to pass up this perk while you're saving for your year off. You're probably used to receiving a certain amount in your paycheck after the 401(k) deduction is made. Your goal should be to save from that take-home pay rather than giving up your 401(k) benefit. If you eventually decide that a year off isn't right for you, you'll have given up a great deal of money in taxes and in contributions from your employer. Furthermore, if you drop out of a retirement savings plan, you may be passing up hundreds of thousands of dollars that will accrue over the years.

Obviously, your 401(k) will be put on hold during your year off, unless your employer continues to pay you. Therefore, the last thing you need is to damage it further by not utilizing this benefit while you're saving for your year off. We'll discuss in Chapter 4 how important it is to refrain from raiding your 401(k) during your year off.

When you drop out of the 401(k) plan offered by your employer, you're not really biting the bullet to save for your year off. You're simply robbing Peter to pay Paul. Saving for a year off takes a lot more discipline than just walking up to the Human Resource Department and dropping out of the savings plan.

You need to keep that retirement savings program intact. And you also must start a new savings account. As we discussed in Chapter 2, you need a separate and distinct year off fund. All of the money you save for your year off should be deposited in this account. For your peace-of-mind, it is important that you keep these funds segregated from your other savings. Otherwise, you may inadvertently draw upon your emergency fund or other savings to finance your year away from work.

In all likelihood, your year off fund will be a simple money market fund that you can draw upon whenever you need cash. When you need money during your year off, the last thing you'll need is to pay bank penalties or be forced to liquidate stock at an inopportune time. Nevertheless, some readers will need to invest more aggressively and take more risks to build their year-off fund.

If it will be several years before you can afford to take time off, an aggressive stock mutual fund might be the answer. Look for a highly-rated fund that has demonstrated success over a long period of time. You can minimize the risk through dollar-cost averaging.

With dollar-cost averaging, you invest systematically. After your initial investment, you put away a specific amount at regular intervals in the mutual fund. Because you invest the same amount at fixed intervals, you avoid buying too many shares when the price is high. Your money does, however, purchase more shares in the fund when the price is low. If you faithfully use the dollar-cost averaging strategy, your cost per share will be quite favorable. Therefore, when you liquidate your shares, you should do quite well.

The dollar-cost averaging strategy is for those readers who are years away from taking time off. It is a long-term strategy, well-suited for those readers who will depend more upon their investment success to build a year off fund. Obviously, no one should undertake riskier investments with money they can't afford to lose. It is one thing to take chances with your year off fund. Risking your primary savings is a totally different ballgame.

Even though you can minimize your risk with dollar-cost averaging, don't forget one unpalatable possibility. If you invest aggressively, you might end up in a worse position than when you started. Years from now, you may be as far away from a year off as you are now.

Most readers will not want to wait years before taking time off. Their savings will be in conservative and liquid investments. They will not need dollar-cost averaging or volatile investments to build their year off fund.

In either case, building and maintaining a year off fund will be your first exercise in self-discipline. If you're constantly tapping it when the mood hits you or you're short of cash, this fund will never be available for your year off. You have to keep your hands off this account if you ever hope to take a year off.

SAVING FOR YOUR YEAR OFF

Setting up a year off fund is the easy part. Building it to a level where it can sustain you for a year is another matter. Maybe you can fill up on those little bags of nuts in the airline club and save the per diem money your company gives you when you're traveling on business. Seriously, you'll need to look at all your expenses, small and large, and eliminate as many expenditures as you can. The money you save must go immediately into your year off fund.

There's a line in *The Big Chill* where Richard, played by actor Don Galloway, remarks that he makes a good living. He jokes that he almost makes as much as his family spends. The truth, however, is that many people do, in fact, spend every penny they earn.

It's sort of like the Peter Principle which says that you rise to the level of your incompetence. Many people's spending rises to the level of their income. They were doing quite nicely with a particular spending pattern. Their income rises and somehow they begin spending the additional money in their paycheck.

When you're saving for a year off, it's imperative that you reverse those spending habits. You should be banking the extra money in your paycheck, not increasing your spending accordingly. If you get a raise, the extra money should go immediately in your year off fund. Any bonuses, incentive pay, or unexpected cash from your employer should be funnelled into that account.

If you earn more than the maximum taxable wage base for Social Security, the later months of the year are happy ones for you. You'll see more money in your paycheck because the FICA (Federal Insurance Contributions Act) taxes stop. The extra money in your paycheck should be deposited in your year off fund.

These FICA taxes will also be important in deciding when to take your year off. We will discuss this timing issue at length in Chapter 13.

There won't always be extra money in your paycheck to save for your year off. You're going to have to slash your budget and slash it again. Even when you're finished saving for your year off, your budget won't go back to normal. You'll need to stick with this bare-bones budget during your year off. Eventually, you'll grow accustomed to living on less and won't view it as much of a sacrifice. If it is too much of a sacrifice, having a year off isn't very important to you.

Cutting your budget is a lot like dieting. Once you reduce your budget, you can't go on a binge and spend freely. There's no yo-yo budgeting allowed when you're preparing for your year off. You can't cheat on that budget either, after you've embarked on your sabbatical.

Just as it is with dieting, the goal is to change your lifestyle. Saving money should become painless as you realize that time off is a great deal more rewarding than many of the purchases you make. Who knows. Maybe you'll even change your eating habits and your spending habits.

You might be worried that your diet will go out the window during the year off. Perhaps, you fear you'll be buying unhealthy or fatty foods to save money. With the right planning, you can stay on your diet and save money at the same time.

You can eat a late lunch out instead of a more expensive dinner. If restaurants in your area offer early-bird dinner specials, you can treat yourself instead of eating late which is tougher on the waistline. And if you're a careful shopper, you'll find that you can buy healthy foods on the budget you establish.

It helps to keep in mind that you aren't really giving anything up. You're simply adjusting your lifestyle to save money. Although there are many sacrifices required to take a year off, watching what you eat or eating at a different time of day shouldn't be difficult.

Initially, you should track your pattern of spending over the past year. Look at how much you spend each month and determine where you can cut down. Distinguish between payments you have to make like the mortgage or utilities and discretionary spending. You have control over your discretionary spending and can cut it significantly. Even monthly obligations like utilities can be cut by turning down the thermostat or by watching the long-distance calls.

Whether you're taking a year off or not, pay off your credit card debt. Saving for a year off is difficult enough without paying 15 percent or more in interest on the unpaid balances. Although having credit will give you some flexibility during your year off, these cards should all be paid off in the initial stages of planning for your year of freedom.

Look closely at your family's debt-to-income ratio. If it's high already because of your mortgage and car loans, saving for a year off will be more challenging. As a general rule, your loan obligations for each month should not be greater than 37% to 40% of your gross monthly income. Reducing debt and your monthly payments will help you during your year off, as well as during years to come.

As you analyze your spending patterns, you'll easily see where the problems lie. Maybe you're spending far too much on clothes. Perhaps, it's not the obvious purchases that are causing you problems like an $85 silk Gucci necktie. You may be buying more modestly-priced items, only too many of them.

If you honestly believe your wardrobe for work is inadequate, try a consignment store or resale shop for a change. You might even try not buying any clothes for a few months and wearing the ones you have. Life as we know it probably won't come to a halt if you stop buying clothes, although the stores you usually frequent might be sorely disappointed.

There are books and magazines that outline hundreds of ways to save money. You can make purchases in flea markets, use coupons, shop wisely, make things yourself, do your own repairs, or a thousand other possibilities.

Those seemingly insignificant expenditures can add up. Get used to pumping your own gas and washing the car yourself. Cut down on your trips in the car and start walking. When you must drive, make your trips cost effective by combining your errands.

Make the library one of your stops. You can read your newspapers and magazines there to save money. Don't buy any books you can check out of the library, unless it's this one, of course.

Bartering can help you save money too. Keep your eyes open for situations where you exchange your labor for the services you need. In a recent newsletter, a writer offered literary evaluations in exchange for repairs to her house.

You can save more than just money. When you're on those business trips before your sabbatical, save those complimentary drink bottles. (You'll never get to take a year off if you spend your money paying for them.) When you're at the hotel, hang on to those toiletries you get for free in the room. You'll save money and they'll come in handy if you travel during your year off. Although you don't need to become obsessed, remember that every dollar you save reduces the time until your sabbatical.

Before you make any purchase, you might ask yourself if it's more important to you than taking a year off. Few purchases will meet that standard, if you're serious about wanting time off from work.

As you make a concerted effort to save money, it's absolutely necessary to take these savings and deposit them in your year off fund. Otherwise, you risk spending them in a moment of weakness. In addition, as you watch your year off fund grow, you'll receive the gratification you need to keep making these sacrifices.

Obviously, it will take saving on a larger scale to finance a year off. If you're a two income family, try living on one salary and banking the rest in your year off fund. If only one working spouse wanted a year off and the family could live on one salary, taking a year off wouldn't be all that difficult. The challenge, however, is arranging a year off for both spouses, if that's your situation.

Another way to save for a year off is to make more money. That may be a totally unpalatable option, if you're already overworked and spending no time with your family. It's an option to consider, however, if your dream for the year off is another career or to pursue a money-making hobby. Perhaps, you can engage in some of those activities, earn additional money for your year off, and gain some experience at the same time.

SUMMARY

Before you can experience a year off, you'll need to develop discipline and self-control. You need to channel your frustration and anger into a positive solution. Before you lose another night's sleep, get started.

Set up a separate year off account that's liquid and safe. If you're counting on investing to save for a year off, opt for an aggressive mutual fund and use dollar-cost averaging to minimize the risk. Even riskier investments are unlikely, however, to finance your year off and may delay your sabbatical.

Cut your discretionary spending in half. Bank all windfalls from birthday gifts to bonuses, along with extra money in your paycheck. If you're a two-income family, try to live on one for an extended period.

Look into ways to make extra money. If you moonlight, work in an area that you want to pursue during your year off. Make certain that surplus income goes immediately into your year off account.

You won't find the key to taking time off on some infomercial in the middle of the night. There's no 900 number you can call for guidance. As your year off account grows, however, you'll sleep a whole lot better.

FINANCING YOUR YEAR OFF

You probably have a mental picture of how you'll finance your year off. You'll be standing at the exit ramp of the freeway with a sign that says, "Will work for food." Or you'll be spending your days roaming the streets, looking for aluminum cans to sell at the recycling center for forty cents a pound.

Hopefully, you'll be able to come up with a better way. In Chapter 3, we talked about ways to cut expenses. Cutting expenses isn't enough.

In Chapter 3, we talked also about saving for this year off. For most people, that won't be enough. Therefore, in this chapter, we'll look at ways to finance that year off, assuming again that your employer won't offer any form of salary continuation. In this chapter, we'll get down to the nitty-gritty of paying for your year off. And if you remember that expression, chances are you're long overdue for time off.

What you're trying to do is to turn a dream into reality. A recent poll of office workers found that 69 percent daydream of quitting their job. Maybe you daydream about being rich and leaving the work force behind.

A dream is different from a goal. While you may dream of chucking it all forever, there is a different approach that's far more realistic. You can set a goal of taking a year off.

TIME OFF AND HOW TO GET THERE

Only you really know how far away from a year off you are. You've got the figures in front of you and know what your financial position is. Your finances may be in terrible shape and you don't have much in the bank. Maybe, your debt-income ratio is bad.

Whether you're a short distance from the goal line or a football field away, let's look at how to reach it. Suppose it takes $50,000 per year for you to live comfortably but not lavishly. And as a starting point, let's say your take-home pay is $50,000.

After you've gotten into the saving mode we discussed in Chapter 3, you are able to live on $40,000. After one year, you've saved $10,000. But even better, you're only $30,000 away from your goal. Because you're now living on $40,000 and have saved $10,000, you're $30,000 away from the goal after one year.

In theory, you can shave another $5,000 off your budget during the second year. Therefore, you've shown you're capable of living on $35,000 per year. Since you saved $15,000 during the second year, you now have $25,000 in your year off fund. After the second year, you're only $10,000 away from your goal since you've proven you can live on $35,000 per year. In theory, your year off account would be funded in less than three years.

Obviously, there are flaws in this theoretical approach. If you operate on a bare-bones budget now, it will be impossible to trim that much fat from it. Cutting your discretionary spending won't yield anywhere near the amount you need. Not many of us would be able to live on the $6,000 per year budget that one gentleman in Seattle survives nicely on.

A second flaw in the hypothetical is that most readers won't be able to wait three years to take time off. Taking a year off requires patience but not that much patience. Don't bank on investment income for a large percentage of the amount you need for your time off. Even if you invest aggressively as we discussed in Chapter 3, it's quite unlikely you'll build the appropriate nest egg needed for your particular situation.

In fact, it may take at least four years for the dollar-cost averaging strategy mentioned in Chapter 3 to work effectively. Jane Bryant Quinn, the financial expert, estimates that it takes four years for the market to collapse and recover. Consequently, dollar-cost averaging or any investment strategy must be utilized over the long term. And it's hard to think long term when work is sucking the life out of you.

The return on your investment may barely keep up with inflation. Instead of relying on investment income or interest to build the nest egg you need, view it as a cushion to cover the incidental expenses you may have missed in your budget. No matter what amount you need in your year off account, you can achieve that goal by utilizing a number of approaches.

UTILIZING YOUR HOUSE TO YOUR ADVANTAGE

We've already established that you don't want to sell your home to finance this year off. It may, however, be an asset you can utilize to help pay for your time off. Let's look at some of the options.

Initially, think about how you'll be spending your time off. We've already touched upon some of the possibilities. You may want to travel extensively or work in a resort community. While you're traveling the globe, basking in the sunshine, or communing with nature, your house may be going to waste.

If your year off plans take you away from home, renting your house can solve many problems. Let's assume your mortgage, taxes and other expenses are $1500 per month. Even when you're not there, the checks are due each month. Renting your house can offset those expenses and might even leave a few dollars extra. Any rent you get means you'll need that much less to pay for your year off.

If you've been a homeowner for awhile, you may not realize how attractive your house is as a rental property. Since you're not going to take your furniture along on your travels, you might get an even better price. Plus, you'll keep building equity in your home and get a few tax breaks. Even if you just break even, it certainly beats a situation where you're paying all of those expenses, along with the cost of traveling.

If you own a so-called executive home with luxury features, you might be able to rent it for far more than $1500. You'll also help avoid some of the problems we discuss in Chapter 10. Someone will be living in your home, so you won't have to worry about frozen pipes or the dangers of an unoccupied house. You won't need to depend on a trusted friend or relative to check the house daily.

Nevertheless, renting your house can create a totally different set of problems. As an absentee landlord, you still might need to call upon friends and relatives for assistance. In the alternative, you might utilize a rental management agent or rental manager. The fee for this service will be roughly three to eight percent of the annual rent.

If you get a bad tenant, you might be aggravated for the duration of your time off. Make sure you verify employment by asking to see W-4 forms or last year's federal income tax return. Run a credit check on the prospective tenant. Ask for a large security deposit. And so your attorney can afford to take time off someday, make sure the lease won't cause you problems.

Even if you're staying in town for a year, renting your home can help finance your time off. You can trade down for the year. In one major metropolitan area, a $100,000 home in a nice area rents for $1500 per month. Fifteen miles down the road in a small town, a nice two bedroom apartment in a safe neighborhood rents for $300 per month. Taking time off might be worth the trade-off of living more modestly, especially if your travels will take you away frequently.

Obviously, if your dream for time off revolves around the house you live in, this is not an option. Your dream may be to work in your woodshop more often or spend more time in the garden. You may want to use the basement for your model railroading hobby or to build miniature dollhouses.

Or perhaps you own a vacation home that would pay for your time off, if you sold it. Once again, if your dream sabbatical involves spending more time there, it's not a piece of property that you'll liquidate to build a year off fund.

In either situation, renting your property doesn't fit the bill. Furthermore, if you can't stand the thought of anyone spilling food on your couch or soaking in your bathtub, this is not the way to go. If, however, you can live with the idea of strangers in your home, we'll discuss these and other options in Chapter 11.

But don't despair. You can still finance your year off, without renting or selling the house. There may be other assets you can liquidate to pay for your year off. No, I'm not suggesting a giant garage sale where you sell everything to build your nest egg for the year off. Nevertheless, you can scale down your life-style in exchange for time off.

CASHING OUT

Faith Popcorn, author of *The Popcorn Report*, predicts that people, even those individuals who aren't financially secure, will be cashing out in the 1990s. Popcorn anticipates that they will sell everything and start over to find inner peace.

Paul Terhorst, author of *Cashing in on the American Dream: How to retire at 35*, suggests selling your house and other assets so you can leave your job behind. We're operating from the premise that you don't really want to sell your house. But there are other options.

As a jumping off point, ask yourself if you really need that second car. We've talked already about how your commuting costs will diminish if you leave work. When you don't have to go back and forth to work each day, that second car might be a luxury you really don't need.

Obviously, you'll save money if you sell that second car. Even when you don't drive it, a car depreciates with each month that you keep it. Although your premium drops when you drive less, you still pay a high insurance bill, even when the car is sitting in the garage most of the time. If you're still making payments on the car, you're being socked each month for interest, along with the amount you owe toward the principal.

More importantly, however, that second car is an asset you can liquidate to help finance your year off. Unless your second auto is a Jaguar or Mercedes 560 SL, selling the second car is only a partial solution but it will help your year-off fund grow. Whether you cut down the family auto fleet or start driving economy cars, you're on the road to time off.

Unfortunately, you may be driving a Geo Metro and not a Miata down that road. If you can't do without a second car, you can trade down. Driving a reliable economy car shouldn't diminish your enjoyment of a year off.

Maybe there are other assets that you don't enjoy nearly as much as time off. Perhaps, there's a piano that no one has played since the kids stopped taking lessons. Or you might be a boat owner who only takes it out twice per season. These underutilized assets can be liquidated to partially finance your year off.

Clearly, you wouldn't think of touching these assets if your year-off plan revolves around activities involving them. If your dream is to take piano lessons or boat more during your year off, you'll need to look elsewhere for assets you can part with.

Maybe, as you exit the fast lane, some of the trappings of wealth aren't as important to you as they once were. It's something to think about when you hear that radio ad which promises cash for your Rolex watch. Perhaps, all you really need for your year off is a waterproof watch for those weeks and months at the beach. For a year, you might not even need a watch.

To get your year off fund started, you don't have to part with high-ticket items like pianos or boats. Take a look through that closet to see if there are any clothes you're no longer wearing. We talked in Chapter 3 about buying clothes in consignment shops to save money. These resale shops may also help you make some money.

Your clothing will be sold for about 25 to 50 percent of its retail value. Normally, you and the consignment shop will split the proceeds when the item is sold. As a word of caution, don't sell those business suits yet. You may need them upon your return to the work place.

It's not just clothes that can help you pick up a little extra cash. There are resale shops that specialize in used sports equipment. Those skis you used twice before the broken leg might fetch a pretty penny.

Maybe that several thousand dollar stereo system is wasted on your tone-deaf ears. Besides, if you rent your house, the tenants may break it. Ask around to see if there's a market for that fifty inch television that set you back $2,000.

As you go through the house, do an inventory of your possessions. The inventory will come in handy for insurance purposes, if you ever have a problem. It can also help as you prepare for your year off. There may be many items buried in the attic that will come in handy during your year off.

Many families own collectibles that are only gathering dust. There may be a stamps, coins, comic books, or baseball cards that can be sold to put toward your year-off fund. If you hope to pass on those collectibles to your children to keep in their attic, other sources of funding must be considered.

Go on an expedition to the land that time forgot, your attic. Maybe there's an old train set up there or even an old Barbie doll, which now is a collector's item.

Start reading up on the marketability of those assets, so you'll get full value for them when you liquidate. Take your collection to several dealers, so you'll know if they're offering a fair price.

HAPPINESS IS POSITIVE CASH FLOW

Boardroom Incentives, a company in Springfield, New Jersey, sells T-shirts featuring the words of venture capitalist, Frederick R. Adler. The T-shirt proclaims, "Happiness is positive cash flow."

Unfortunately, you are not going to have positive cash flow during this year off. There will be more money going out than coming in. You'll be drawing on your savings, not watching your bank book grow. Your nest egg will dwindle each month and that's a difficult adjustment.

The separate and distinct year-off account solves many of the psychological problems. As we've mentioned, this is an account that is over and above your regular savings. As you calculate your net worth, this account should not even be viewed as an asset. Therefore, when you're drawing upon it during your time off, your traditional assets aren't being depleted. Your cash flow springs from an asset that exists solely for that purpose.

If you have trouble keeping positive cash flow now, you're going to encounter problems, whether you take a year off or not. When you have trouble living on a paycheck, living without one is going to be difficult at best. Once your year off account is fully funded and your time off begins, you'll withdraw the amount you've budgeted at the intervals you've chosen. Those dates will be the equivalent of payday. And if you're withdrawing more frequently than you planned, it's just as bad as failing to live on your paycheck.

Going into debt to finance a year off doesn't produce positive cash flow. Taking out loans is no way to finance a year off. Borrowing money is not a palatable option. When you get a second mortgage or borrow with a home equity loan, you're putting your house on the line. This makes taking a year off even more dangerous than it might be otherwise.

Despite the advertisements you hear and read, home equity loans should not be the source of funds for your year off. You might ask why, since these advertisements tout home equity loans to pay for dream vacations. Unfortunately, that alone may be a bad piece of financial planning advice.

Even if you fall for the advertisements that push home equity loans to pay for dream vacations, there's one important difference. Taking a year off is much more costly than a dream vacation, unless you're taking a cruise around the world or a lengthy trip on the Concorde.

Another problem is that when you take a dream vacation, even if you take out a home equity loan to pay for it, you're coming back to a paycheck. When you take a year off, you're not coming back to a regular salary for at least one year. And in the worst-case scenario, you may have some difficulty finding a comparable paycheck again.

Although a home equity loan should not be used to finance your time away from work, you should apply for a home equity line of credit while you're still working. This line of credit can be an excellent safety net if you find it difficult to reenter the work force after your one year sabbatical.

If you wait until during your year off to apply, you might find it more difficult to qualify. Therefore, establish this home equity line of credit before you take time off and your income flow diminishes.

Obviously, you should find a bank that doesn't charge interest until you draw upon the cash reserve. Many financial institutions offer promotions where you can sign up for the home equity line of credit without paying any points or closing costs of any kind.

Although going into debt to pay for a year off is dangerous, refinancing isn't a problem as long as you don't increase the amount you owe. It will put additional cash in your hands right now, if the rates are lower than they were when you took out the loan. It will be less money each month that must be paid out.

Don't make the mistake of going for a longer mortgage to decrease your monthly payments. The idea with taking a year off isn't to put you in hock for a lifetime and delay your eventual retirement.

You'll need as much cash as you can get during your year off. It should be readily accessible in an account you can withdraw from without penalty. You'll need ready access to your funds to replace the money you aren't getting in your paycheck.

Your money must be in liquid investments. Otherwise, you'll be liquidating assets at what may be an inopportune moment. You could wind up selling stock or some other asset at the point when its value is the lowest.

TAPPING THOSE LONG-FORGOTTEN ASSETS

Chances are, you've lost track of some assets. Maybe, there are shares of stock that you've been meaning to sell. Some forty-year-old readers will find they still hold shares of stock that relatives gave them under the Uniform Gift to Minors Act. If it's the right time to sell and the tax ramifications are negligible, sell them and put the proceeds in your year off account.

Dig up those savings bonds that you got for your bar-mitzvah or confirmation. As you'll see in the timing chapter, these savings bonds can be cashed during your year when your income is low. The tax ramifications won't be nearly as bad as they would be if you cashed them in during a peak income year. Some of these bonds may be so old, they're not earning interest any longer.

Stay away from those savings bonds you're accumulating for your child's college fund. There's a tax break on those and you can't justify robbing your child's college fund to take a year off.

Tempting as it might be, keep your hands off the 401(k) and Individual Retirement Accounts. The penalties for raiding them are severe, unless you're 59 1/2.

If you are forced to quit to take time off, it is imperative that you roll over those funds into an IRA. Otherwise, the tax implications are enormous and you'll be mortgaging your future for time off now. Nevertheless, a small portion of your savings may have been taxed already. That money doesn't need to be rolled over and can be applied to your year-off fund. Check with the benefits administrator at your place of business and see what the rules are.

Don't think you can just convert your family's emergency fund into a year off account. The three to six month emergency fund recommended by most financial planners is over and above the money you need for your year off. If you've taken the drastic step of quitting to get time off, you may need that emergency fund if there are problems reentering the work force. Now if you were saving for the Hummer superjeep driven by Arnold Schwarzenegger and others, you can deposit those funds into the year off account.

You need cash during your year off. That might mean borrowing from any life insurance policies you have with significant cash value. While you're at it, cut your insurance premiums wherever you can so that you'll have more money in your pocket. Raise the deductibles wherever possible.

Whether it's a dollar or a thousand that you're putting away for your time off, get it into the year-off account. Otherwise, you may be tempted to use it to support your current life-style.

TWO CAN LIVE AS CHEAPLY AS ONE

How does that old cliche go? Two can live as cheaply as one. "Sure thing," you say. "We may both live in the same house but we don't wear the same clothes or drive the same car. Two may be able to bathe as cheaply as one, but that's about it." Nevertheless, if you're both going to take a year off, you'll need to live as cheaply as possible for awhile.

In Chapter 14, we'll discuss the impact of taking a year off on your family. If you come from a two-income household, you can work toward the goal of banking one salary in the year-off account. As we discussed in Chapter 3, banking one salary helps you save for your time off. And during your year off, one salary will pay for it, once you're accustomed to living at that income level.

To get down to specifics, here's how to get used to living on one paycheck. If your employer has direct deposit, put down the book and go sign up. Put one paycheck directly into the year-off account, whether it's a mutual fund, money market account, or savings account.

If you're the only bread-winner in the family, begin a forced savings program immediately. Sign up for $100 or more to be automatically deposited in the year off account each month. This is called paying yourself first and you'll have to, if you hope to get time off.

Even if you had no plans for a year off, you should be saving at least ten percent of your pay. Twenty percent or more should be manageable, if you hope to finance time off. You should continually set new goals on how much you're saving.

When you get a raise, increase the amount you save.

You're obviously managing to get by on what you're making now, so bank the increase in pay. If you don't get used to seeing it in your paycheck, you'll never miss it. Regardless of whether you want time off or not, never overextend yourself in anticipation of a raise you may not get.

If you've sold the second car to raise cash or have paid off a car loan, there should be more money available to save. As loans are paid off, increase the amount you save accordingly. If you managed to pay $200 each month on a car loan, you can bank that amount once the car loan is paid off. Nevertheless, make allowances in your budget for car repairs as your automobile grows older.

Obviously, if you're building a year-off fund exclusively by saving money, you'll need to bank a lot more than $200 per month. As noted above, even aggressive investing isn't going to help.

Even if you can only swing $100 per month, the most important thing is to get started now. Whether you want to take time off a year from now or five years from now, don't procrastinate.

MAKING MONEY DURING YOUR TIME OFF

Some readers have decided that they don't just want to contemplate the meaning of life during their year off. If you plan to make money, no matter how little, it can help finance your year off. Whether you plan to make money or not, it's best to have enough saved to live on without it, in case your money-making endeavors aren't as profitable as you anticipate.

If you're shooting for an entry-level job in a new career

field, don't bank on making much. Let's say your dream is to host a radio talk show. Chances are, you'll find yourself in some small town, making $125 a week while you learn the business. The money you're earning won't go too far in financing your year off.

Another problem is that you may have more trouble getting an entry level job than one that's comparable to your present position. A potential employer will question your commitment and may not be open to an applicant who's making a career change later in life.

That outdoor job you've yearned for may pay very little. And unless it comes with room and board, the salary won't solve the problem of financing your year off.

As a starting point, take a look at Jeffrey Maltzman's book, *Jobs in Paradise*. It offers tips on landing your dream job. Of course, you may view paradise as a place where no one works, especially you.

It's unlikely you want to work just as hard as you do now during your year off and make one-tenth as much. For many readers, it will be ideal to work part-time or occasionally at some fun job where there's little stress or pressure. Since any money you make should just be the icing on your year off fund, have fun with it or don't keep the job.

Maybe, you can work as an extra on a movie. The pay is terrible but it's something different. Perhaps, there's a golf tournament or some other event where you can pick up work for a few days.

To many, the thought of working during their year off is totally unthinkable. It's as distasteful as our earlier suggestion that you moonlight to make extra money for your sabbatical. If you feel this way, you'll need to finance your year off in one of the other ways we've suggested.

Although moonlighting while you're still working may add considerably to your stress, it does have one advantage. It can open the door to a more profitable endeavor during your time off.

Instead of moonlighting, maybe you can increase your current income in another way. If you're on commission, push a little harder to get one more order this month. Make those extra follow-up calls with the goal of taking time off in mind. Hopefully, it will result in extra money that you can put into your year off fund.

SUMMARY

If time off is really important to you, you're going to lose your customer-of-the-month status at the Sharper Image. In fact, you may even be selling some of those Yuppie toys to finance your time off.

As you prepare for your year off, you'll need to conserve cash, wherever possible. To fund and preserve your year-off account, you'll need to zealously watch your spending. Cut your discretionary spending, wherever possible. Even your budget for food, clothing, utilities and other necessities can be curtailed to a large extent.

If your dream is to play golf at the country club every day for a year, you'll need a lot more money for your time off. Those cart and greens fees can test any budget, even if you are working. Nevertheless, if you can hack the public courses, you'll make it with money left over for ugly pants to wear.

To fund your year off, you need to liquidate assets you

don't use. Since selling their house is not a viable option for most readers, consider the other alternatives like renting it while you're traveling or living elsewhere. Consider trading down to a less expensive home during your year off.

Your year-off account need not be at a bank. You might have your money parked in a no-load growth mutual fund. The danger, however, is that the market may not cooperate with your plans for a year off. You may be forced to sell your shares when they are at a low point.

As we'll see in the timing chapter, certain investments like savings bonds can't be cashed in until you're in a lower income tax bracket. Therefore, your money won't be physically in the year-off account until your time off begins. Consequently, with certain investments like stocks, there is a risk that your portfolio will be worth less than you think at the time it's liquidated. If you anticipate the price per share will drop, it's better to sell now even though the timing for income tax purposes isn't necessarily right.

When the time comes for your year off, the bulk of your funds should be in an account that you can tap at any time without penalty, whether it's a bank, credit union, or money market fund. You need to know how much you have and feel confident your money is accessible at all times. You don't want to be at the mercy of a volatile investment.

Before we took our sabbatical, I used to keep a running total of the funds in our year-off account on an index card in my shirt pocket. On the way to work each morning, I would look at it and feel a little better about the day to come.

CAREER DECISIONS

Before looking at the career implications of taking a year off, it's important to ask yourself one important question: Does your career infringe upon your personal life? "What personal life?" one executive asked.

And that's how many employees feel. Their job cuts deeply into any free time they have.

Vacations aren't necessarily the answer. Many employees find it difficult to get away from work. They know they'll return to an even larger pile of work upon their return.

Former 49er football coach, Bill Walsh, stated that you can only stay in the pressure cooker so long before you require a sabbatical. And the only way to get that sabbatical is to quit.

So the question becomes: How do you get a break when you're ready to crack? One answer is clear. After you crack, you'll get a break and may never be permitted to return to your job.

There's no doubt that the choices are painful. One middle manager for a large corporation said it all. "I need a break from my job," she said. "I need to just not work and see what it's like. I'll worry about a job later. And if I don't like it, I'll go back to work. I just need the opportunity to find out if I'll like it. But I've come too far to give it all up."

And that is the danger. Sure, someday you can go back to work but it may never be the same. Because of the white-collar recession, you may never be paid the money you're making now or have the same stature.

For some people, work is so intolerable, they hope to get fired. And at some point in your life, you may be forced to take a year off or longer involuntarily. Unfortunately, an involuntary separation is totally different from time off that's carefully planned and anxiously awaited. When you take a year off involuntarily, you often spend your time looking for another position which is a full-time job in and of itself.

Some people hope that the choice is someone else's, not theirs. When they leave work under those circumstances, they feel it's fate rather than a conscious decision they'll come to regret later. While that may help some cope better, you are not in control of the situation. Furthermore, your time off may come at a point in your life when you really don't want or need a sabbatical. Rather than waiting for someone else to make the decision for you, taking a year off requires decisive action on your part.

Employers with vision are few and far between. A supervisor for an insurance company went to her boss with a simple question. "I've been here for four years. My husband gets six weeks off. My kids are off for the Summer. I only get two weeks vacation and won't get three until next year. Is there any way I can take a few days off without pay?"

Her boss frowns. "We've never done anything like that," she says with a sneer. Worse yet, the woman making the request feels her boss now has a negative impression of her.

For this woman and many others, the pressures are enormous. Along with their demanding jobs, many women work at what has been called the "second shift." They work another forty hours, taking care of children and the house.

As you consider whether to take a year off or not, keep several points in mind. First of all, no one's indispensable. You won't necessarily be missed, except by the four people who borrow your newspaper each morning and the guy who raids your candy jar.

Be aware too that there are plenty of people who'd be glad to have your job. There will also be plenty of competition for any others that you want. Consequently, if you can arrange to take time off from your current job with a guarantee of employment afterwards, ask where do I sign. Nevertheless, even with this alternative, there are potential problems.

CAREER INTERRUPTUS

As too many women have found out, interrupting one's career is extremely dangerous. As the example above indicates, perception is one major problem. Anyone wanting time off is viewed as having priorities that may be inconsistent with the good of the company. From that moment on, the individual's commitment may be questioned.

The February 10, 1993 issue of the *Wall Street Journal* reported on one study. Researchers found that women who leave the work force temporarily experience an average 33 percent drop in wages when they return. Furthermore, their pay never catches up with women who continued working.

The person taking time off faces other problems. He or she may lose seniority, earnings, and training. His or her skills may become rusty or obsolete.

The risks of taking a year off get greater as you grow older. It may be especially difficult to get another job, if you opt to take a year off despite your employer's objections. The sad reality is that older workers often find it more difficult to reenter the job market. Furthermore, pension benefits might be adversely affected.

It's a year when you're not contributing to your 401(k) retirement savings plan. Perhaps, this will mean you'll live less comfortably in your sunset years. Of course, if what we're reading is true, many of us will feel the need to work again when we're in our sixties and seventies. For most readers, the risk of having to work part-time when they're in their sixties or seventies is one they can comfortably assume at this time.

Throughout your career, you've taken risks. Taking time off may be the biggest risk you've ever taken. As you make your decision, keep the old maxim in mind: Never risk more than you can afford to lose. If you can't afford to lose your job, the risks are too great.

Before taking any risk, it's imperative that you know what you want. Even if you know what your dream job is, that won't necessarily solve all of your problems. You may not be qualified for the job, don't have the talent, or can't break into that field.

Let's say you want to be a Hollywood screenwriter. Even assuming you have the talent, the competition is fierce and it helps to have contacts. Therefore, career decisions aren't as simple as saying, "This is what I want to do with my life."

Sometimes, economic factors dictate the decisions we make.

Maybe your dream is to work in radio or television. Are you willing to pay the price of success? Maybe you paid a steep price in your present career and are just now reaping the rewards. You may not have the energy to start at the bottom again.

If you truly wanted to be in radio, you would be willing to work anywhere, even if it's at a 10,000 watt radio station in an area of the country that you wouldn't want to drive through, let alone live. You'd jump at any television opportunity, even if the station was in Frostbite Falls, Minnesota. Assuming your age didn't work against you, you'd be willing to start in the mailroom and take years to move up the ladder.

Most of us know what we don't want to do with the rest of our life. And it may just be that you don't want to spend another day at your present position. Although that certainly is a career decision, it's only one of many issues you must resolve before taking a year off.

You need to be aware of the dichotomy that exists for many people in terms of their career. The dichotomy is illustrated by a two-pronged question that must be answered. If you were independently wealthy, would you still work at the same job? The answer is probably "no." The second half of the question is: If I'm not independently wealthy and have to work, would I stay with this job? And for many, the answer is "yes."

Unfortunately, this is the level of job satisfaction at which many people work. If they didn't have to work, they'd quit tomorrow. But since they do have to work, their position is palatable. Obviously, in an ideal world, you'd get paid a good buck for something you love to do.

These are some of the issues you can explore at length during your year off. You can decide if the career you chose ten or twenty years ago is still satisfying, if it ever was.

You can see if that dream job exists, the one that gives you satisfaction while paying a sum of money on which you can live comfortably. To arrange this time off, however, you may lose the job you hold now which is at least marginally satisfying, either emotionally or financially.

Once again, you have to look at yourself to see if you're equipped to deal with the potential harm a year off can bring. It's easy to say, "No guts, no glory." Still, there will be many who will be sorry they risked what they have now for a year off, especially if their new career doesn't meet their expectations or if they have difficulty reentering the work force.

In the dozens of articles you read about people who willingly or were forced to leave their job, there is usually a positive focus. They opened a successful business or found true contentment in a simpler life-style or career. You won't read much about those individuals who regretted their decision and were sorry about what they left behind. In retrospect, their old job didn't seem so bad.

Comparisons like this are unavoidable. You're making decisions that can change your life, and it won't always be for the better. Whether your year off turns out to be a satisfying experience or a mistake, you must decide if you're content with the way your life is now or if you'll shoot for something more. You're at the fork in the road, just as you are with any important decision. The results may be negative, but you'll at least have taken your shot. Somehow, that seems a lot better than always wondering.

ABSENCE WITHOUT MALICE

We'll deal first with the happier possibility which is that your employer will agree to the leave of absence. Even in this situation, there are some very negative possibilities.

Very few employers will guarantee a return to the same position you left. In most cases, you'll be assured of a comparable position. Although the salary might be the same, the comparable position won't necessarily be as prestigious. If you're anxious for a change and have been stuck in the same position for years, your bigger fear is probably that you will return to the same job. Nevertheless, as we'll see in Chapter 9, there are dangers for those who are promised a comparable job and you should negotiate a resolution of this issue in advance.

As mentioned above, even when you are granted time off, you may be looked at differently forever. By taking time off, you may slide off the fast track. For many, however, the fast track lost its luster years ago.

An associate at a law firm may be permitted to take a year off, with or without pay. From that moment on, however, the attorney may not be viewed as being on the partnership track. Although the leave of absence was granted, it was not without malice.

There may always be a subtle bias against the employee who takes time off. The bias remains beneath the surface and there is never any overt sign that it exists. It's similar to what occurs when an employee relocates because of a spouse's job situation. The company may always view the employee skeptically from that point in time forward.

Even if you're granted time off, you may sustain a break in service. You may have to work a full year, before regaining all of the benefits you have now.

DAMAGE CONTROL

If your employer has nixed the year off, you face the ultimate choice: Is a year off worth losing my job over? A magazine production editor in Manhattan asked for a six-week leave of absence so she could volunteer to work in Israel. When her request was turned down, she quit.

The truly frightening possibility is that you'll be taking more than a year off, if you quit to get it. Even though your financial preparation should allow for some cushion, saving for more than a year off is extremely difficult.

An eighteen month or longer job search is not beyond the realm of possibility. Your financial well-being can be seriously jeopardized if as cash runs short near the end of your year off, you face another year in search of employment.

To find work, you may be forced to relocate. This is a bigger risk for some than others. If you're in your dream house now or live near aging parents, you may be totally unwilling to relocate. Therefore, quitting to take time off is even riskier.

If you've made the decision to take the plunge, even though your employer won't guarantee a position upon your return, you have to look at the realities of your individual situation. Look first at your age. Sadly, the older you get, the less marketable you become. There is still a subtle discrimination against older job applicants. Remember, too, that a potential employer may have a different view of what constitutes old, no matter how young at heart you feel.

It's not just your age that can cause a problem. Employers may not be enthusiastic about the one-year gap in your resume. Furthermore, many job experts believe you're better off looking for work while you're employed. Potential employers view you more favorably.

When your year off is over, you may have trouble convincing potential employers that your separation was voluntary. At a minimum, obtain references before leaving your current employer and make sure the letters explain the circumstances surrounding your departure.

Perhaps, you can show a potential employer that your time off is a positive attribute. Let that company know that it gave you the time to decide what you really want and this new job is it. Point out that your batteries are recharged and you're ready for a challenge.

Check out those Labor Department projections for your job category. You'll have a clearer view of the employment picture facing you in a year. Nonetheless, even if you work in one of the hot career fields for the 1990s, there's no guarantee that you'll find a position easily after your time off.

Economic data won't help you get a job. Even if the

economists are predicting a robust economy, it won't necessarily mean a hill of beans to you. Still, this information should be factored into your decision. If you work on Wall Street and thousands of your co-workers are being laid off, the chances of your finding a job are bleaker. Similarly, if you work in the banking industry and scores of jobs are being lost due to bank mergers, the odds are against you coming out of the year off unscathed.

We'll talk in Chapter 8 about the dress rehearsal concept. Test the water now by sending out resumes. It's one way to test your marketability.

In the movie, *Baby Boom*, Diane Keaton's character is offered the chance to work again in the City. Don't bank on your being extended the same offer. It may be an uphill battle to regain your present stature.

To put a positive spin on the potential damages from taking time off, let's consider one other element in the equation. Unlike in years past when employees worked for the same company throughout their career, the times they are a-changing, to quote Bob Dylan. It's quite unlikely that you'll have job security throughout a lengthy career and you eventually will become disposable. If you must leave to get time off, it's doubtful you're leaving a position that would be yours forever.

SUMMARY

Interrupting your career to take a year off is certainly risky. On the other hand, if you're ready to hand in your notice today, taking a year off after carefully weighing all of the risks is a far more rational course of action. Nevertheless, you need to do more than just pipe dream about taking time off. You must move forward toward that goal.

There's an old saying that goes something like this: Life is what happens while you're busy making plans. It's time to plan for your year off and do something about it.

DON'T TELL YOUR EMPLOYER YET

It's Monday morning again. Nothing's changed much since Friday. It's the same old same old. The same papers are piled up in your office. The ones you got rid of before are back in some other form. You're being nagged by the same people with the same problems. It makes you want to scream.

Control those impulses. The timing's still not right. You still have some preparatory steps.

Admittedly, that's difficult when your calendar is filled with the same pointless meetings. Your schedule is jammed to the gills again. You're facing meetings to resolve issues raised at last week's meetings. And next week, you'll need more meetings to clarify decisions made this week.

At lunchtime, you thumb through the book, *The 100 Best Companies to Work for in America*. Not so surprisingly, you don't see your employer listed. If Robert Levering and Milton Moskowitz ever write a book, *The 100 Biggest Sweatshops in America*, you fully expect your employer to be at the top of the list.

Maybe, some readers' employers are named as one of the best companies to work for in America. Nevertheless, if you work for one of those companies and aren't happy, you're probably wondering how your employer made the list. Despite your skepticism, based on the book's criteria, you're employer has been judged to be better than most. Whether your employer's listed or not, you can use some of the same criteria to do your own analysis. Levering and Moskowitz use pay/benefits, opportunities, job security, pride in work/company, openness/fairness, and camaraderie/friendliness. It's important to evaluate your situation, so you won't do anything rash and just quit.

Joni Mitchell once sang: "Don't it always seem to go. That you don't know what you've got 'til it's gone." When you're evaluating what you might lose if you take a year off, it's a decision that must be made with full awareness of the risks.

You may not be able to duplicate your present situation, if your need for a year off forces you to quit. *The 100 Best Companies to Work for in America* talks about more unusual benefits such as $3 haircuts or a week's vacation for newlyweds. Living without perks like that won't be a problem. Losing health insurance or some other indispensable benefit, however, can devastate your family.

That's why, if at all possible, you should attempt to arrange your year off with your employer's blessing. Unless you want to spend your year off looking for another job, and believe me it might take at least that long, a sabbatical from your present position is the way to go.

It's tough to accept that statement when you're in the middle of another miserable day at work. You're at your wits' end and every piece of gray matter is telling you to quit. Obviously, you'll feel this way on many occasions as you take the preparatory steps toward your year off. As much as you want to go in there and get it off your chest, it has to wait.

Hating your job alone isn't reason enough to take a year off. More than likely, the same problems will exist upon your return. Furthermore, taking a year off isn't designed to make a statement to your employer. Don't harbor any false illusions that your bosses will realize how foolish they've been and will beg you to stay. When you do tell your employer, your goal is to arrange the most favorable terms you can, not throw a fit to show how mistreated you've been. You must approach your employer with a strategy for arranging a year off.

LET YOUR FINGERS DO THE WALKING

Before you walk out in a huff, dust it off or dig it up. If you work at a larger company, there should be an employee handbook or a benefits book. The answer might be in there.

Or maybe there's a manual that contains the company policy on sabbaticals or leaves of absence. You need to find it to see if the employer is under any obligation to grant your request for time off.

If the policy is in writing, you can also find out some other important information like whether you're entitled to credit for service or seniority during your time off. Examine the policy to learn how benefits are handled during the time away from work.

Depending upon the reasons why you want a year off, the policy may cover your situation. There may be leaves for personal growth, social service leaves, or extended personal leave.

A small number of companies pay an employee's full salary, so he or she can volunteer for a worthy cause. If community service is what you have in mind for your year off, there may be a company policy that compels your employer to look more favorably upon your request. A policy of this kind results in good PR for the employer. It also helps the employee develop skills and contacts that ultimately will benefit the employer.

One company allows unpaid sabbaticals for employees who run for office or go back to school. Unwinding or vegging out isn't a satisfactory reason for taking time off.

Perhaps, your state has passed employment legislation that offers some relief. Take a look at the Family and Medical Leave Act which became effective on August 5, 1993 and applies to companies with fifty or more employees. Study it to see if it's applicable to your situation.

The unwritten rules are important too. Investigate whether anyone's been granted a leave of absence and why. If you work for a large company, find out what's been done in other departments. There may be a precedent for what you hope to do.

Look at the political environment too. Your boss may not be able to fill your slot, because of a hiring freeze. Be cognizant of the levels of bureaucracy. Consider those up the chain of command who need to approve your leave of absence.

Take a good look at your employer's track record when it comes to flexibility. Is there a flexible hours policy? Is there job sharing? Are employees permitted to work out of their home? Or is there resistance to any innovative program? Perhaps, it took years for your employer to implement a dress-down day, long after other companies were letting workers wear casual clothes on a certain day each month. If there's no flexible working environment now, the reaction to your request for time off is likely to be negative.

Looking beyond the written company policies, you can analyze how your employer reacts to change. You may even be able to predict your boss' reaction. He or she will say, "This is the way we've always done it. If we do it for you, everyone will be running in here, asking for time off."

Before you even mention your desire for a sabbatical, you must fully consider the implications for your employer. When you're ready to negotiate, a subject we'll discuss thoroughly in Chapter 9, you must be ready to address your employers' concerns. Until then, your desire for time off is none of their concern.

SUMMARY

With a little luck, you'll receive the same support for your sabbatical as one attorney did. His firm allowed him to take a sabbatical so he could train for the Iditarod, a 1,163-mile dog-sled race through the Alaskan wilderness. Staff members of the firm even helped raise money to finance his participation in the race.

Now there's an idea. Maybe your co-workers will throw a fund-raiser to finance your year off. Don't bet on it. Whether you're entering a dog-sled race or spending a year with the family dog, don't expect a favorable reaction from your boss.

Until you've considered all of the ramifications of taking a year off and have devised a plan, you shouldn't breathe a word to your employer. And come to think of it, you shouldn't even mention it to your co-workers. In most offices, word will get back to the boss before you've even decided whether taking time off is right for you. As a result, you may jeopardize your status, even if you decide against it.

It would be great if you have a trusted friend in Human Resources who knows where the skeletons are buried and can point you in the right direction when you're searching for information. Unfortunately, however, you're risking that your plan will leak prematurely.

You may find that your company will be breaking new ground, if it grants you a sabbatical. At all but the most progressive companies, ground is broken reluctantly if at all. Because of this, you won't bulldoze your employer into granting the sabbatical. You need to consider the advice in every chapter and work out every detail in your plan before approaching your employer.

You must hold off on telling your employer anything, until you know exactly what you need to take time off. It's not a case of seeing what you can get from the employer and working from there. You'll be working from now until retirement, unless you patiently devise and execute a plan for taking time off.

There's a wonderful poem in James Autry's book, *Love and Profit*. It reads as follows:

They leave a lot out of the personnel handbooks.
Dying, for instance.
You can find funeral leave
    but you can't find dying.

You can't find what to do
    when a guy you've worked with since you both
    were pups
    looks you in the eye
    and says something about hope and
    chemotherapy.

No phrases,
    no triplicate forms,
    no rating systems.
Seminars won't do it
    and it's too late for a new policy on sabbaticals.

BABY STEPS
TOWARD TAKING
A YEAR OFF

You wake up in the middle of the night. You're having those nightmares again and they all involve work. Maybe, in your dream, you've missed another deadline or told off your boss.

Or, perhaps, your dreams are more subtle. In the *USA Weekend* section, a reader described his dream. He's at the wheel of a speeding station wagon. He has no idea where he's going and can't control the speed of the car. The brakes of the car are virtually useless. It takes all of his strength for the man to steer the car. The man wakes up exhausted with his heart pounding.

The dream is analyzed by an expert from the Jung Center in Maine. She indicates that work pressures are responsible for the dreams. Increased pressure at work is making the man feel like he doesn't have control.

Whether your dreams are easy to interpret or not, there's no question that work can give you nightmares. On the other hand, your job might be giving you insomnia. Night after night, you lie awake worrying about problems at work. Your stomach is in knots from aggravation or dread of some unpalatable situation.

If the situation gets worse, you may need to talk with Dr. Grant, the radio psychologist. Even if you don't have a sleep disorder, Dr. Grant offered some good advice that applies to those who dream of taking a year off. Dr. Grant advised that baby steps are a good way to reach a goal. And there are baby steps that you can take to reach the goal of taking a year off.

SIMON SEZ TAKE TWO STEPS FORWARD

We've talked before about some of the preliminary financial steps you can take. You can set up a year-off account and begin funding it. You can work to get out of debt and pay off your high-interest loans. Enroll in a forced savings program that automatically puts away money before you get your hands on it. Create a budget and stick to it. Track your spending over several months and see where your problems are.

Start stockpiling the items you'll need for your year off. Each week, you should be getting coupons in the mail or in the newspaper for free items like toothpaste. These are the perfect travel sizes for your year off. Although these sample sizes aren't economical to buy, they're perfect when they're free.

Similarly, stock up on the recreational items you'll need for your year off. Maybe you'll find them at a garage sale on a Saturday morning. At least, it will keep you out of the mall.

You can begin exploring those alternative careers that seem so much more fulfilling than your present job. If your dream is to become a photographer, take a night school course and devour every book on photography you can find.

Make it a point to read every publication that can help you learn more about the field in which you want to be in. Read *Variety* or *Backstage* magazines, if it's show biz that intrigues you. Take an acting class or participate in a local theater group. Go to a few auditions to see if your hide is thick enough to cope with the process.

The lawyers in one city put on a musical each year for charity. In this fashion, frustrated script writers, musicians and thespians can get a taste of the life they hope to lead during their year off.

Most communities have a cable channel that's hungry for any type of program. There's ample opportunity for you to take baby steps and embarrass yourself in front of the entire neighborhood. Of course, this would presume that anyone ever watches the community access channel.

A small-town dentist moonlighted as a sports talk show host. Fortunately, he listened to the old advice, "Don't quit your day job." After a short stint on the air, his career as a talk show host came to an abrupt end.

You aren't going to walk into a dream situation without some baby steps along the way. One hard-working accountant does taxes by day and plays piano in a jazz trio at night. If he takes a year off to pursue other musical endeavors, he'll be far more prepared than the amateur musicians who only dream of doing more with their music.

For some of them, the dream job was advertised in the Sunday *New York Times* on October 20, 1991. A restaurant on the Caribbean island of St. Martin was looking for a piano/vocalist to play Broadway tunes.

Whether it's St. Martin, Oklahoma, or the South Pacific that you want to travel to during your year off, you can take baby steps to get there. Brigadoon is probably out of the question, but map out your plans anyway.

Plan the itinerary for your year off. Hit the library for *Foder's* and every other travel book. Develop a travel budget you can live with during your time off. Save those frequent flyer awards, hotel certificates, and coupons for free rental cars.

If you intend to live somewhere else during your year off, begin subscribing to the newspaper from that location. Find out if there are any job opportunities, if you need to make some money during the year away from your regular career. Use the newspaper to learn about rental prices and real estate values.

Although they're just safe little baby steps, you'll learn from them. You'll find out if the activities you've planned for your year off will be satisfying. You'll also move a little bit closer to the day when you can take time off.

TIME OFF: EXCURSIONS AND DIVERSIONS

You should be taking baby steps toward your goal, not getting sidetracked along the way. It's easy to justify a diversion from your routine as preparation for taking time off. If you lack the discipline to work toward that end, you may rationalize that you're just taking baby steps.

The danger is that these diversions cut into the funds you're saving for time off. Let's say you've seen the Robert Redford movie, *A River Runs Through It,* and dream of spending a year off fly fishing. Instead of moving slowing toward that goal, you take the easy way. You spend five days at the L.L. Bean fly fishing school in Maine. You're now several thousand dollars further from your goal, even though you claim this was a baby step toward achieving your dream.

You need baby steps and a dress rehearsal as we'll discuss in Chapter 8, but don't confuse them with this situation. Instead of reading up on fly fishing or having a friend show you the ropes, you've chosen instead to escape from your present life-style under the guise of baby steps.

Or maybe you head for Captiva Island in Florida for a learn-to-sail vacation. With every excursion, you drift further away from the time when you can take a year off.

Although a certain amount of travel is necessary in preparation for your time off, it should only take place after your plan for taking a year off is nearing completion. The motorcycle tour of Europe may be great but it doesn't move you closer to your goal. Don't be a baby about it. You're working toward a longer and more rewarding excursion.

SUMMARY

You'll never reach the goal of taking a year off with just baby steps. Nevertheless, it's time to get started and accelerate your pace later on.

Because of the hectic life you lead due to work, finding time for these activities is difficult at best. Unless you take these baby steps, however, you'll never be able to swing a sabbatical or utilize it fully. It's too late for baby steps, after you're committed to a year off.

No matter how small the steps are, you will be making progress toward the goal of taking time off. All of these steps have a secondary benefit. With each baby step you take, you should be better off financially and intellectually, even if you're never able to arrange a year off.

On a chilly and dreary day in Pittsburgh, I spotted a sporty little car driving through the city. The driver looked to be in his mid-thirties. On the back of his car was a bike rack and a ten-speed tied securely to it. On the roof of the car was a kayak. And in the car, you could see paddles and other recreational equipment.

The driver of the car may have been in the midst of a sabbatical or a week off. Or maybe he had just taken some baby steps toward a year off. Whether he was leaving that day or years later, his car was packed and ready to go.

DRESS REHEARSAL

After a grueling day at the office, a woman trudges toward the bus stop. A ragged man with a sign crosses her path. "The world will end in three days," he screams at her. "I hope so," she says and continues on to her bus stop.

You know your career's hit rock bottom when you're forty years old and the television commercials for the military look inviting. "Be all that you can be," they sing as they're jumping out of planes and you're humming along with them.

Meanwhile, back in the real world, you're getting up at 5:30, working twelve hours with twenty minutes for lunch, attending meeting after meeting, and arriving home at 6:30 except on those days when an accident has brought traffic to a halt. On those days, quality time with your family begins at 9:00 in the evening.

Like the commercial says, "it's not a job, it's an adventure." It's an adventure all right, an adventure in boredom. Or if you're in a career like nursing or law, it's an adventure in stress. The closest you come to real adventure is when you're skidding out of control down the large hill near your house on an icy Winter day.

You might be a little long in the tooth for the military, but there are more exciting careers than yours. Author, Alex Hiam's book, *Adventure Careers*, describes exciting jobs like deep sea diving or bungee jumping.

We talked before about the movie, *City Slickers*, which dealt with some mid-lifers who sought adventure vacations to make up for their dreary jobs. There's a lesson to be learned from Billy Crystal and his friends. If your dream is to become a cowboy, try out a cattle drive first.

Seriously, the point is that exciting jobs look better from afar. Similarly, a year off from work may also look better from afar. You might want to try out that adventure career or your time off, before making an irreversible commitment. And that's where the dress rehearsal comes in.

UP GOES THE CURTAIN ON A YEAR OFF

Taking a year off is a lot like the situation faced by many when they retire. Some people retire and then regret it. A study for the National Institute on Aging shows that the number of retirees who reenter the workforce has doubled. With workers retiring at a younger age, retirement becomes a less permanent option. That isn't a problem, unless you're unable to find a job comparable to the one you left, if that's your preference.

An engineer for a Fortune 500 company almost made a terrible mistake. He was convinced that he hated his job and nothing could be better than driving an eighteen wheeler. An acquaintance stopped him in the hall and wished him luck when she heard he was quitting. She found out that he was back already, albeit in a new position, after quitting.

After two days behind the wheel of his truck, the engineer hated it. Fortunately, his employer rehired him, but in a different position from the one he left. The engineer found that new job to be even worse than the one he left, but better than truck driving.

Although you're only taking a year off, you need to have a detailed plan for how you'll spend your time. And you need to do a dry run to see if there are any bugs in your plan. This dress rehearsal would certainly have been an eye opener for the engineer who wanted to be a truck driver.

Let's say you're planning to turn a hobby into a business during your year off. Maybe you learned how to make leather belts during the sixties when you thought about joining a commune. Twenty-five years later, you're not up for joining a commune, but you'd still like to make belts and sell them.

Even though you're not chucking everything to take a year off, you need a trial run with this life-style. There are ways to simulate the year-off experience, before you go full steam ahead with your plan. If it's belt-making that you hope to pursue during your year off, devote as much time to that hobby as is humanly possible before approaching your employer.

In other words, before committing to a year off, take your hobby to the next level. Immerse yourself in all aspects of the hobby, so you'll get a taste of how you'll like it as a full time endeavor. Treat it as a business instead of just a hobby. This means handling the bookkeeping, accounting, marketing and other details that go hand-in-hand with running a business.

Start spending weekends selling the items you make at local craft shows. Better yet, spend a few weeks living out of a trailer going from craft show to craft show. Find out if all facets of the business are appealing. Deal with the public at those craft shows, instead of just working on your belts. See how well you cope with customers haggling over the price of your belts or if you can deal with snide remarks about your craftsmanship. You'll have put your plan to the ultimate test, after a few bounced checks and a craft show where it rains for the entire weekend.

If it's a writing hobby you want to work at during your time off, do more than just dabble in it for a month. Maybe now, you send out a few query letters each month. For at least a few weeks, devote the same amount of effort that you'll exert when your time off arrives. Send out a hundred query letters instead of just a few. Find out if the results are encouraging enough to take a year off. And if not, make sure you're capable of persevering in the face of rejection.

To the extent possible, simulate the writing environment in which you'll function. If you picture yourself in a rustic cabin in some remote location, try it out for at least a week. See if your creative juices flow or if you're stir crazy after a few days.

An ad for a rental in *Poets & Writers Magazine* paints this picture: "Writer's cottage on mountain sheep farm. Snug, remote, secluded, achingly quiet. $100 a week." Although the price is right, you might find that the "achingly quiet" surroundings are more than you can stand.

In contrast, you may have the dream of writing in a beach environment with your computer overlooking the ocean. The dress rehearsal may show you that a dream climate isn't necessarily conducive to your writing. You may need structure in your day and fewer distractions than what you'll find in a beach community. After a few hours in the sun, you may find that a nap seems far more appealing than writing.

As a teenager, you couldn't do your homework with the television on. Similarly, you may not be able to get anything done when there's a golf course or beach volleyball game nearby. Even if you're going to live where you are now, you may find that working out of your home offers too many distractions.

FINANCIAL DRESS REHEARSAL

All of this talk about dress rehearsals brings to mind a story about a man and his clothes. We were talking to a friend who sells shoes in Bloomingdale's. A well-dressed man came in to the department to purchase Bally's, even though the alligator shoes he was wearing looked perfectly fine. He was wearing what our friend estimated to be an $800 suit. The customer proceeded to buy a pair of $225 shoes and paid cash. He put the new shoes on and took the "old" ones with him in the box.

Before the customer left, our friend introduced us and mentioned that we were taking a year off. We joked that we now wear plastic shoes from Picway. The customer graciously told us we'd live longer, thanks to the time off.

Clothes and the other trappings of success are important to many people. Everyone has priorities that govern the way he or she spends money. Some people who earn $20,000 per year think nothing of buying outfits that others making $100,000 would view as too rich for their blood.

When you spend money, and lots of it, you can justify the outgo in many ways. There are a host of rationalizations you can use such as: My career demands it. I have an image to maintain. I've earned it. Life's too short to cut corners.

Short of therapy, there's no telling why you feel this way. Maybe you felt deprived as a child and overcompensate now. To take time off, you'll have to overcome these feelings and develop a new attitude toward spending money.

During your year-off dress rehearsal, your attitude toward buying clothes and all your spending habits will be tested. If these habits are too ingrained to change, you'll never be able to break them so you can take time off. To succeed at taking time off, you need to learn if you can perform your part night after night.

Your budget needs to be put to the test. If you're going from two incomes to one during your year off, start now and try it out. You may become sick of it. More than likely, however, you'll realize that a more Spartan existence is still a very good one. If you rely on one income, start living on the year-off budget now. You'll save money and find out if you have the financial discipline necessary for taking a year off.

As long as this financial dress rehearsal continues, you'll be bolstering your year off account and that can only help your situation down the road. The dress rehearsal can reveal the flaws in your financial preparation. And if you can't execute your plan now, it's not going to get any better during your year off.

LIFE-STYLE DRESS REHEARSAL

You don't want to risk your career on a dream that hasn't been road tested. From afar, certain life-styles look wonderful. They also look less expensive than they might be. Before making an irrevocable commitment, there are ways to test the water.

It's almost like the process of buying a vacation or retirement home in a resort area. The biggest mistake many people make is that they buy right away without thoroughly investigating the area and the wide-range of housing options. They wind up in a home that doesn't meet their needs.

The condo that looked so good initially turns out to be too small as a full-time dwelling. Although it may be great as a one-week vacation spot, the home is too far from shopping and other activities that are an integral part of a non-vacation existence.

The home on Martha's Vineyard or Nantucket seems to be a dream life-style when you're there for a few weeks in Summer. As an all-year round home, however, it may be too expensive or too boring during the off-season. Or maybe it's the opposite. During the Summer season, it's too congested and you can't wait for the off season.

Lee and Saralee Rosenberg, co-authors of *50 Fabulous Places to Retire in America*, point out a common mistake which they call the Disney Syndrome. People think that a place where they enjoy vacationing is perfect for year-round living. It's one reason the Rosenberg's recommend renting for six months or a year before buying a piece of property.

The wrong time to find this out is after you've sold

your primary dwelling. At that point, you may have already sold your furniture and the possessions of a lifetime. Many people benefit by making a gradual transition to a different life-style or home in a different area. In South Florida, thousands of snowbirds come down for the Winter before deciding whether they want to become full time residents.

An extended dress rehearsal can help you avoid finding out about these problems when it's too late. It's akin to a situation that develops when people buy a time-share investment. After a year or two, they grow tired of returning to the same area but are locked in to that particular investment. At that point, however, they are unable to unload the time-share or trade it for a vacation that interests them more.

Before taking a year off, you need a trial run. Taking two weeks of vacation in a particular area probably isn't enough. You'll still have that tendency to view your time off as a vacation and not a life-style. If the cost of living is high, you're more likely to overlook the expense because you still have a paycheck coming in.

The life-style dress rehearsal needs to include at least a month of the worst that your location has to offer. If it's Florida, spend some time there when it's terribly humid and buggy during the Summer. Even if it's the so-called dry heat of Arizona, try it in August when it's 110 degrees.

A life-style dress rehearsal requires longer than a few weeks. Perhaps, you can adjust to the key elements of your new life-style while you're still working. If you work for a national corporation, maybe you can transfer to that area of the country instead of taking your year off to go there. Even if you can't relocate to the exact area that interests you, you'll still be a lot closer and can spend more time there. You'll be hedging your bets instead of risking it all on a dream you've never tested. You might even get some assistance with relocation expenses.

If your plan is to travel during your year off, you might also be able to test the water through your present career. There may be overseas assignments available or positions that require more exotic travel than you're getting now. Granted, business travel is nothing like traveling for pleasure, but it does create opportunities to experience the life-style. Better yet, you might even collect enough frequent flyer miles to do some real traveling during your year off.

Or perhaps you'd like to do volunteer work and put some meaning back in your life. Many large corporations have programs which let employees take time off for good deeds. Start there and see what happens.

SUMMARY

Basketball broadcaster, Al McGuire, suggested that the coach of the Chicago Bulls should take a sabbatical. McGuire commented in August 1993 that Phil Jackson, the coach, appeared tired. A visit to Jackson's off-season retreat in Montana wouldn't suffice, said McGuire.

"I mean, who the hell can live in Montana?" McGuire asked. "The first 48 hours are beautiful. But after that, the mountains don't move."

Al McGuire notwithstanding, you might be able to stare at the mountains in Montana for a year and never tire of them. But you can never be absolutely sure. And before you commit yourself to a year in the middle of Montana or any mountainous region, no matter how picturesque, you need a dress rehearsal of longer than 48 hours.

To summarize, there's a great deal you can learn from the dress rehearsal. You'll find out if you've budgeted correctly. You'll see if hobbies are as much fun on a full time basis. You'll learn how your family will react to spending more time with you.

As we'll discuss in Chapter 14, there are different issues involved in households where both adults work. If you and your partner decide to take turns taking time off, the person who goes second can have the ultimate dress rehearsal. He or she can get a first-hand look at the pro's and con's of taking time off.

But here's another possibility. Consider using the year off as a dress rehearsal for retirement. You may learn a great deal about what retirement is like, before it's too late.

And here's one last thing to practice before deciding that it's worth losing your job to get a year off. Practice looking for work for a month or two. Find out how marketable you are and how much rejection you'll face. If it bothers you now, think about how you'll deal with it when you don't have a job to fall back on.

Dr. Grant, the radio psychologist, was fond of saying, "Life isn't a dress rehearsal." But before you spend a year of your life away from work, you need a dress rehearsal.

JUDGMENT DAY

The movie, *City Slickers*, told the story of a group of friends at mid-life who were tired of their boring jobs. Every year, they would take an exciting vacation to break the monotony. During one vacation, they ran with the bulls in Pamplona, Spain.

The movie, however, dealt with their current adventure which was to participate in a cattle drive.

One of the characters summed up the feelings of many people who will read this book. He says, "At this age, where you are …you are." And that's scary for many.

Where they are is at a job they hate. On the way to work each morning, they see the billboard for Windsor Canadian whiskey. It says, "Fortunately, every day has an evening." The message is that even though you have to go to work, at least you can come home each night and have a drink.

If the only thing you enjoy about your day is having a shot of whiskey at the end of it, you need a different book than this one to help with your problem. For the sake of your liver, I hope there's a different carrot you can dangle to get you through the day. And that's an extended period when you can take a year off from work.

Once you're convinced that a year off is right for you, it's time to approach your employer. No matter how good you are at thinking on your feet, you need to be thoroughly prepared for your meeting. You must approach your employer with a list of options. And you must know how far you're willing to go to take time off. Ultimately, you might be forced to quit to get time off.

I'M WALKING

If you're an all-pro running back, it's easy to say I'm walking, unless you meet my demands. He also has a professional agent to negotiate for him.

Chances are, you don't handle negotiations for a living. Some readers will be good negotiators and some won't. No matter how good or bad you are, it all comes down to leverage. And only you know how much leverage you really have.

Bill Waterson who created *Calvin and Hobbes*, arranged a nine-month sabbatical in 1991. Cartoonists like Gary Trudeau of *Doonesbury*, or Gary Larson of *The Far Side*, had a great deal of leverage when they asked for time off. The public loves their cartoons and the syndicates that distribute their work derive a great deal of income from them. In addition, while Larson took time off, newspapers used previously run material.

The premier cartoonists have another advantage. They have a source of income while they're away from work. Unfortunately, you may not have anywhere near the leverage or the money of a successful cartoonist who wants time off. In fact, only a handful of cartoonists have the leverage needed to negotiate a sabbatical.

Legendary money manager, Peter Lynch, was welcomed back with open arms after he left Fidelity Investments for an extended period. He now works part-time for the company. His replacement, Morris Smith, left Fidelity after two years to spend at least a year in Israel. The company gave him an open door for when he wants to return.

If you're a middle manager which some claim is an endangered species, you may have little leverage at a negotiating session. Your boss may be feeling the pressure to cut back people in your position. Although that won't mean much for you in the way of leverage, you'll see that the pressure on your superiors may play into your hands.

Whether you're a middle manager, a lawyer, or in any occupation where there are too many bodies and too few positions, you possess special talents and experience that your employer values. Otherwise, you would have been gone long ago. More than likely, your employer wants to keep you, if only because no one has the time to train someone else to do the job.

Before you approach your employer, you have to look at your value to the organization. Check your last performance appraisal. Was it glowing or did you barely meet the minimum requirements for the position? Unless there is a clearly defined policy established regarding sabbaticals or personal leaves of absence, your success will be dependent upon how the organization views you. If your performance is viewed as mediocre and you're not perceived as adding value to the organization, you'll definitely have a tough time at the negotiating table.

Obviously, a company will do more for a prized employee. Rules are and will be bent, if you're viewed as someone who's performed in an exemplary fashion. The star employee will always have leverage in any negotiation.

If you're viewed negatively by your bosses, their eyes may light up when you talk about leaving. Your employer may suspect you'll leave of your own accord, if the sabbatical isn't granted.

Clearly, the more you have to offer, the better chance you'll have of taking time off. If you haven't performed up to your potential over the past few years, there's still hope. As you take the preliminary steps toward a year off, take on additional challenges, learn new skills and accept more responsibility. If eventually you decide a sabbatical isn't the right choice, you may get your career on the right path, if that's what you want.

Many readers may not be viewed as highly as they should be, through no fault of their own. Perhaps, there is a personality conflict or bad blood between you and your boss. If this is the case, your leverage may be more unusual. Approach the employer and be blunt about your differences. The year off can be offered as a way for both parties to get a fresh start. During that year off, the employer might come to appreciate your contributions to the organization. Better yet, your boss might move on to greener pastures while you're gone.

Even if you're certain the year off is the right move for you, don't tip your hand when approaching your employer. As is the case in any negotiating session, you need to play your cards discreetly. If you are planning to explore alternative careers during your year off, you're not going to want to spill the beans to your employer. After all, the company wants you to return in a year not subsidize your search for self-fulfillment.

In arranging time off, there are a number of possibilities. You could ask for a year off, with pay or without. Perhaps, you'll settle for something less than a year with partial pay. Some readers will be satisfied if their employer guarantees to hold a job for them or is willing to keep benefits intact during the leave of absence.

Ideally, on judgment day, there will be a genuine arms-length negotiation with your employer for time off. Nevertheless, in the real world, some employers will do no negotiating. Your supervisor may suggest that you take the rest of your career off. Too many employers will view the employee as just another body that can be replaced and they'll be able to muddle through without that person.

You can't be too prepared for this bargaining session. Anticipate your boss' concerns and come up with solutions to those problems. Role play with a trusted friend or relative.

Stick with the issue at hand, time off. Don't whine about your pay or working conditions.

Have fall-back positions and be flexible. Decide if you're willing to consider anything less than a year off. See if your boss will consider letting you take time off on a trial basis. Obviously, that will make it more difficult to make plans, but there's less risk associated with this option.

Decide in advance if there's anything else you're willing to give up. Are you willing to be available for phone calls and questions, within reason? Are you willing to stop by to answer questions? Would you agree to work a day or two a month? Can you work on a long-term project that won't interfere with your time off?

There's also a negotiating technique called going for the extra mile. Even if you're satisfied with your employer's offer, go for a little more. It can't hurt to ask. You may just get that little extra sweetener.

Finally, in any negotiation, know your adversary. Will your boss agree to time off but blame his superiors when your request is denied? You have to know if your boss will fight on your behalf or just go through the motions.

Your boss may have a totally different set of values than you. He or she may be a workaholic who can't comprehend why anyone would want time off. Your boss may be locked in financially and will resent your being independent enough to go without a paycheck for an extended period.

THE UPSIDE OF DOWNSIZING

It's easy to be negative about taking a year off. One person expressed this opinion: "In a down economy, people aren't worried about taking a year off; they're just happy to keep their job."

Whereas many people feel they're lucky to be working, they aren't necessarily happy. As the companies they work for become leaner and meaner, these employees have more on their plate. And as one benevolent employer said to a harried employee: "If you have too much on your plate, get another plate."

The down economy can have an upside. A bad economy can present you with opportunities. A great many companies are forced to scale back. If your employer is facing hard times, you may be able to take advantage.

The sabbatical may look more appealing to an employer who is facing lay-offs. Your year off may save the employer from a difficult decision. Paying you less than your current salary for a year may look quite appealing. And paying you no salary may save the employer from laying off a valued employee. From the employer's perspective, business may pick up by the time you return or it may lose employees through attrition.

Granting you a year off can cut costs for some companies. Separation pay for a discharged employee could be significant. In addition, when you and your employer reach an agreement on a year off, it is one less termination that might result in litigation. The employer doesn't have to worry about a wrongful discharge or discrimination suit.

Your plans for a year off may also help the employer avoid more sleepless nights. Downsizing is traumatic for everyone involved, including the person who must give the bad news. An employer may leap at the opportunity to reduce staff, albeit temporary, without the devastating impact of a layoff.

There is precedent for the proposal. American Telephone & Telegraph initiated a leave program in 1992 to reduce salary costs and layoffs. 90,000 managers with five or more years of service were offered unpaid leaves with benefits of nine to 24 months. They were promised a job of like status and pay when they returned.

In February of 1993, General Motors took an unusual step to cut its white collar payroll. Workers were offered fully paid leaves of six to fifteen months, depending upon the length of their service. The catch, however, was that the workers were obligated to quit at the end of their leave.

In early 1992, *The Philadelphia Inquirer* initiated voluntary programs to reduce costs. Some of the possibilities were unpaid leaves, reduced work weeks and job sharing. The newspaper also offered other options such as voluntary separation and early retirement packages.

For those who are sure they have no desire to continue working for their current employer, the voluntary separation package is attractive. If all else fails and you want time off badly enough, you might consider volunteering to be part of a staff reduction. You may be able to negotiate an excellent separation package. In fact, you might even be entitled to outplacement assistance, job counselling or even tuition reimbursement for training of some kind.

And as many employees who survive a downsizing are finding, it's often better to be the one leaving than staying. Those who remain are left to handle the job of those who leave. The survivors are told, "You may have to work some casual overtime." Unfortunately, however, they were already putting in more than casual overtime, prior to the first downsizing.

There are risks with volunteering to be laid off. Your employer may not need to make cuts in your area and you'll be viewed skeptically from that point forward. Many voluntary separation packages give the employer the right to withdraw the offer. If your offer to leave isn't accepted, you may have jeopardized any opportunities you have for advancement.

When approaching your boss to discuss voluntarily separating, explain why you want to leave. If your feelings toward the boss are one reason why you want to leave, try not to mention it. It is almost always in your best interest to leave on good terms. You may need a reference or might like to return as a consultant.

Take a long range view and don't just grab the quick buck you'll get from a package. With job searches taking longer than ever because of the economy, having a guarantee of employment at the end of your time off will help your mood and your outlook considerably.

LOOK 'EM IN THE EYE AND SEE WHO BLINKS

As indicated previously, you must decide how far you're willing to go for a year off. When you approach your employer, you must know exactly what you want and how much you're willing to give. If you've gotten in shape financially, you should eventually be ready to go for a year without pay, as long as you know you'll have a job to come back to twelve months from now.

That guarantee may be the best package most readers will get from their employer. Nevertheless, there are some sweeteners you can request. Ask the employer to keep your health insurance intact. See if you can avoid a break in service while you're out, which may have an adverse impact on your pension and retirement benefits.

Ideally, the negotiation session will be a give-and-take one. If it appears that quitting is the only way to take a year off, look for a middle ground. Find out if the employer can live with a shorter leave of absence. Perhaps, you can agree to be on call or can come into the office on a monthly basis to handle questions and problems that arise.

Within reason, agree to handle specific projects such

as budgets or some long-term assignment that won't interfere with your time off. In exchange for handling these duties, the employer should offer some pay or benefit as a quid pro quo.

You need to have an action plan to assure the employer that you've taken the company's interests into account. The plan should offer suggestions on how work will be handled in your absence and should ensure that key accounts will get the same good service. Assure your superiors that you are still committed to the company. Let them know that you still want to be a part of the organization and can add value.

Even if the employer isn't downsizing, the company can still benefit. Sabbaticals prevent burnout and recharge an employee's battery. The time away from work can lead to increased productivity and creativity, when the employee returns.

There's one great way to look your employer in the eye and see who blinks. If you already have a new job lined up, you can go to the mat during your negotiations for a year off. You can use that offer as leverage.

You don't even have to mention that you have another offer in your pocket. It's enough to know it's there, as you play your hand with an employer.

If you're switching jobs anyway, bargain for time off in advance. Perhaps, you can arrange a sabbatical of a specified duration after so many years of employment. At worst, try to buy some time before starting your new job. If possible, delay the start of your new job so you get some time off.

SUMMARY: JUST DO IT

This is the point in the book where I'm supposed to give you a pep talk. It's supposed to sound like a Nike commercial and end with, "Just do it." Unfortunately, I'm no Lou Holtz, the Notre Dame football coach who is famous for his motivational speeches. Secondly, you shouldn't be doing anything, until you've considered some of the points made in the remaining chapters. Finally, keep in mind that the year off is not right for everyone and the path is filled with risk.

You are truly at the fork in the road and your life may change for the better or worse. Taking this step to improve your life might also jeopardize the elements of your lifestyle that you do value and would hate to lose.

If you choose to go forward, let's go over what we've learned. You must look closely at your strengths and weaknesses before coming to the bargaining table. Be prepared to make concessions and help smooth the transition. Ask for guarantees that you'll come back to your same position, if that's what you want. Be careful with assurances that don't carry any legal weight. Watch out for promises of a comparable position, whatever that means.

Negotiate now for a severance package, in case a mutually agreeable position isn't available. Be as valuable an employee as you can and you'll have a far better chance of getting time off.

When your financial affairs are in order, you'll always be in a stronger negotiating position. You'll have far more options than you would otherwise.

Remember, however, in any negotiation, don't make

ultimatums you'll regret. It's a tough job market out there and quitting to get time off may be a decision you'll regret forever. It may result in more time off than you ever cared to have.

Employers like to use the euphemism, "rightsizing," in place of downsizing. A rightsizing can be the right time to approach your employer and negotiate time off.

If you're sure a year off is right, remember the Robin Williams line in *Dead Poets Society* when he said: "Seize the day. Seize the moment."

The message from that movie went something like this: Don't let your life get away from you. We're only given a finite amount of time. Use it.

TAKING CARE OF BUSINESS WHILE YOU'RE AWAY

Watching someone else live out their fantasy may be as close as you'll get to seizing the day and the moment. And the entertainment industry has a pretty good idea of what your dreams and fantasies are.

In the movie, *Club Paradise*, Robin Williams leaves bitterly cold Chicago to run a resort in the Caribbean. In *Regarding Henry*, Harrison Ford longs for a simpler lifestyle and decides that being a corporate lawyer isn't what he wants to do.

On the small screen, producers recognize that many viewers are longing for a change. In the television show, *Thirtysomething*, the ad executive played by Ken Olin quits his job so he can spend more time with his family.

And then there's the new series, *Big Wave Dave's*. Three friends finally fulfill their dream of opening a surf shop in Hawaii. One critic commented that it is based upon an eternally irresistible premise: Quitting your job to live in a beautiful resort area.

The notion of taking time off is a variation of that premise. Millions of us would love to quit our jobs to live or work in paradise. Nevertheless, taking a year off is a more realistic alternative for those readers who are afraid to risk everything in pursuit of a dream. Furthermore, taking a sabbatical is the more conservative approach for readers with family obligations and assets they want to preserve.

Because you have assets and possessions that must be looked after, you can't just hop in the car and head off for parts unknown. Unless you're going to renounce all of your worldly possessions, you'll still need to take care of business during your year off. There will be bills to pay and a home to maintain. If you plan to travel during your year off or live elsewhere, taking care of business at home will be a challenge.

ALL'S QUIET ON THE HOME FRONT

Unfortunately, you don't just turn the temperature on the water heater down and leave. The first step is eliminating any services you can do without during your year off.

Call the cable company and cut off your service. It's one less bill to worry about. On those occasional visits home during your year off, you can suffer with fuzzy reception and no HBO.

Discuss your situation with the phone company. You can purchase a more limited service during the time you're away or shut off the phone. If you want to keep in touch with friends or business contacts while you're away, the phone company offers an answering service for a modest fee. You can also have your calls forwarded to another number.

Another option is an answering machine that has

remote access. You can call periodically to get your messages. Be sure to get a toll saver feature. With it, you can save long distance charges. The number of rings lets you know if there are any messages. Of course, it doesn't save you money if there are messages that you could care less about. You'll also find the world is full of people who wait for the sound of the tone before hanging up, which leaves you stuck with the call.

On too many occasions, you'll find a sales pitch on your answering machine. One solution is to stipulate in your own message that sales people shouldn't bother giving a sales pitch, since you're not interested. It also helps if you only call your machine when the rates are low.

Unless you want calls from bill collectors, you'll have to deal with those issues too. If you're going to be in one place for an extended period, you can have your mail forwarded. To avoid delays, the post office will set up an account and forward your mail expeditiously for a fee.

To avoid problems, consider paying some bills in advance. For example, you could prepay your utility bills. Before leaving, you can put $200 toward your electric bill. You'll have a credit from which your monthly obligation will be deducted. If there's a problem in getting your mail, your bill will be paid and you won't be charged a penalty. You'll lose a little interest on your money, but it beats the hassle of protesting an improperly assessed penalty. Prepaying bills before you leave also has psychological advantages as we discussed in Chapter 2.

If you pay on a budget plan, you would know exactly how much to send each month even without the bill. By keeping a calendar of the bills owed, you would be able to send the same amount each month at the appropriate time.

You can arrange to pay some of your bills automatically. Some utilities will automatically deduct the amount owed from your checking or savings account. You need only complete the authorization form before leaving.

Many bank accounts offer a pay-by-phone feature. Assuming you're given an 800 number, you can conveniently pay bills back home in that fashion.

Your insurance company might also be willing to debit your bank account automatically. Some insurers have an automatic debit program that lets you pay your premiums without writing a check, getting a bill, or buying a stamp. After signing up, the amount you owe is automatically withdrawn from a designated account. The statements are sent several weeks before the amount is deducted.

If you owe money on your mortgage or have a car loan, you can arrange for the lender to debit your account each month. In fact, many lenders will give you a break on the interest rate, if you agree to have your loan payment debited automatically.

You can never have enough friends, especially during your year off. You'll need them to check your house while you're away. A friend or relative can be authorized to pick up your mail at the post office. That person can forward the important letters to you.

If you don't want to burden your friends or relatives, there are services in many communities that will check your house for a fee. They'll water plants, flush the toilets, run the water, spray for insects, and do whatever else is necessary when a house sits vacant.

There are also services listed in *Trailer Life, Motorhome,* and other magazines that will receive and hold your mail for you. For a modest fee, these services will send it to you upon request. If you are going to be on the move constantly during your year off, these services will work much better than having your mail forwarded by the post office.

Taking care of your banking can be difficult while you're away. You should try to direct deposit any checks you'll be receiving on a regular basis. If you'll be staying in one area, you should open an account there. You should find an account with few if any fees.

Limit the money you'll be receiving. No, that doesn't mean turning down money. Reinvest your dividends and have your interest checks deposited in your checking account.

Pay as many of your expenses as you can by credit card. Obviously, you'll need a high credit limit. As long as you pay the bills back within the grace period, you won't pay any interest.

Don't take a cash advance on your credit card, unless it's absolutely necessary. You'll usually pay a finance charge right away. If necessary, however, you can get this cash from an ATM. There may be a fee, though, for this transaction.

You might also be able to cash a personal check through the auto club or a credit card company. American Express, for example, will let you cash checks if you have one of their credit cards. The amount you can cash depends upon whether you have a green card, a gold card or a platinum card.

If you have a trustworthy friend or relative, you can give that person access to your checking account. That person can wire money to you, if necessary. Wiring money costs at least $25. Your friend back home can also pay bills on your behalf. Be prepared to return the favor when that individual takes a year off from work. And if you don't cash in your savings bonds before you leave home, remember they're good at any bank in the country.

Unfortunately, you have to prepare for the worst while taking time off. As we'll discuss at length in Chapter 12, take along medical forms and your health insurance information. Find out how your insurance handles medical treatment when you're away from home. See if there are any preferred medical providers in the area where you'll be, so you can limit your out-of-pocket expenses.

Perhaps, a house sitter can solve many of your problems on the home front. In exchange for giving that person lodging, they can take care of many chores around the house. In Chapter 11, we'll talk about ways to keep your house occupied and help your financial position at the same time.

WHO'S MINDING THE STORE?

If you run your own business, you need more than just somebody to watch your house. After years of personally handling every problem that arises in a small business, you're going to find it extremely difficult to just walk away for a year. Chances are, you are reluctant to leave your business in someone else's hands for a week, let alone a year.

Well, at least the boss won't turn down your request for a year off. After all, you know the boss quite well and you couldn't find a nicer person to work for. Realistically, however, most small business owners would find it terribly difficult to take a year off.

Many small businesses are built around the expertise of one person...you. Whether it's a consulting or accounting firm, you're probably afraid your clients won't be there after the year off. You fear they'll find someone else to handle their problems, if you don't provide them with personal service.

No matter what kind of business you own, you're probably handling the lion's share of the duties. Sixty or seventy hour weeks aren't uncommon. Even if you don't want time off, you should be learning to delegate more responsibility so you can break away from the business periodically. Many business owners, however, fear that if they teach employees too much, they'll open a business of their own.

If this fear is lurking in your anxiety closet, your employees should be signing an agreement not to compete. Get your lawyer to draft one that will hold up in court.

Secondly, much of what you're doing yourself can be handled by subordinates. Furthermore, you need to develop employees so they can run the business in your absence. If you become disabled and no one else can fill in, your business will fail.

Business owners have one huge advantage over others who hope to take time off. The boss won't turn down the request. In addition, since your business provides a source of income during your absence, you aren't likely to face the same money problems as other readers will who must take time off without pay.

If you have a partner, taking time off could cause problems. Your partner is likely to be stuck with a great deal more work. One solution is for that partner to receive a greater share of the profits in your absence. Aside from money, your partner may like the idea of getting an equal amount of time off upon your return.

SUMMARY

Even when you're dreaming of taking a year off, a little reality has to creep in. Since we're assuming that you don't want to sell your house and you're only going to liquidate some of your assets, you can't just leave your home unattended. If you're going to just lock the door and leave, you might as well sell your home because it's not going to be worth much a year from now. When you leave your house vacant and unattended, you're asking for problems. There are also insurance problems that can arise when you leave a house vacant, particularly if there's vandalism or frozen pipes.

Unless you take care of business before you leave, problems back home may spoil your travels. And that's not necessarily the only potential glitch in your plans. As the saying goes, be careful what you wish for. It might just come true. There's a danger that your dream activity will be more confining than work.

A lawyer in Wilkes-Barre, Pennsylvania, once

dreamed of owning a sheep ranch in New England and eventually took the plunge. There was a problem, however. He and his wife could never leave, because someone had to take care of the damn sheep. The couple could never leave for a vacation, because someone had to take care of the ranch. Eventually, he sold the ranch and came back to the real world which gave him more freedom.

WHERE TO LIVE AND HOW TO KEEP THE COST DOWN

Oh sure, you're thinking. I'll be able to do a lot of traveling during my year off. I'll be traveling from soup kitchen to soup kitchen.

Or to keep costs down, you can follow the lead of the character played by Robert Urich in the television show, *Crossroads*. In that program, he plays a lawyer who chucks the office grind to ride across the country with his child on a motorcycle. If your backside hurts just thinking about that, there's always the *Route 66* approach which is to travel in your classic Corvette.

Whether you travel by motorcycle, Corvette, or Greyhound bus, keep in mind the warning mentioned earlier. Taking a year off is not a vacation in the classic sense. You can't spend money frivolously and indulge yourself without inhibition.

A study for the Hyatt Hotels and Resorts found that vacations are a time for more sex, food, fun and happiness. Although that's great to a degree, the study reported that executives are more free-spending while on vacation. Many participants forgot about dieting and drank more during vacations.

When you travel during your year off, your main indulgence will be free time. You'll have time for all the sex and fun you can physically tolerate, but you won't be able to spend, eat and drink without restraint. You'll have to indulge yourself in other ways.

Here's the problem in a nutshell. When you work and make good money, you don't have time to travel. During your year off, you'll have time to travel but won't have the same budget you might have otherwise.

In any event, it's quite clear that you won't run into Robin Leach at any of the hotels you're staying at during your year off, unless he's filming at the Motel 6. Nevertheless, you can do some traveling during your year off. Better yet, living away from home can be instrumental in paying for your year off.

TRADING PLACES

We talked briefly in Chapter 4 about utilizing your house to finance time off from work. Assuming you're going to travel extensively, this idea is worthy of further consideration.

Recently, the Beverly Hills home of the late Cary Grant was put on the rental market. The gated 4,000 square foot mansion with its tennis court and pool could have been yours for a mere $40,000 per month rent.

If your home commands that much rent each month, you won't need to be worried about financing your time off. Of course, if you plan on renting Cary Grant's home or something equally pricey, you're back to square one.

Let's look at your present living arrangement and elaborate on the advice we outlined in Chapter 4. Maybe you live in a nice home that you've worked hard to buy. We've talked before that you don't want to sell your house to pay for a year away from work.

Perhaps, however, you are willing to rent it. And if you're willing to trade down, you might be able to help finance your time off.

Suppose you can rent your house and make a little money. The rental income covers your mortgage, taxes and the other costs of home owning. You might even have enough left over to rent an inexpensive but clean apartment in your hometown.

Because you'll be renting your house with furniture and all, you should get more rent. Perhaps, you can rent to a family that's relocating in your town and needs a home for six months to a year. Contact the corporate relocation companies in your town to see if there is a market for your home. If you work for a large company, you may become aware of individuals who are relocating to your area.

Finding someone to rent your home doesn't do you any good, if you're paying the same price to rent somewhere else. After you've put on your landlord hat and negotiated a good price for renting your house, you need to put on your tenant's hat. You must then find an inexpensive rental that meets your needs for the year off.

Living abroad isn't out of the question. As many retirees have found, you can live in Mexico inexpensively. Portugal and Greece offer inexpensive rentals in resort communities. Take a look at Peter Dickinson's book, *Travel and Retirement Edens Abroad*, to see which areas fit into your year off plans.

Your goal is to break even on the costs associated with your primary dwelling. You'll be building equity in that property and getting some tax breaks. During your year off, you'll live in a rental that won't break the bare-bones budget you've established.

One option is to set up a base in a low-cost area of the country that lends itself to the activities you hope to pursue during your year off. Whether it's a farmhouse in Vermont or an apartment in a rural area, you should be able to rent for a song. Although you're trading down for a year to save money, this might be a decent trade-off to get time off. This is especially true, if you're only using your temporary home as a springboard for travel and other ventures.

For some readers, this may present a problem if there are children in a particular school district. We will address more of these family issues in Chapter 14.

Perhaps, you can find a house-sitting opportunity during your year off. Another option is friends or relatives who own vacation homes that they don't use during the off season. You should be able to rent those homes cheaply. The operative word here is rent, unless you plan to mooch your way to time off.

You might even consider going from one off-season rental to another in various parts of the country. It might be a ski resort condo or a South Florida carriage home during the Summer. In any event, you need to find a low-cost rental to make the trade-down beneficial.

If you plan to travel a great deal, you might not even need to rent an apartment. Perhaps, you can simply set up a base at a friend or relative's home for the short periods when you're not on the road. Obviously, if traveling isn't a major part of your year-off activities, living with a friend or relative won't necessarily be palatable.

Finally, make sure you're aware that when you rent your home, you and your tenant are signing a binding contract. If life on the road doesn't appeal to you, your house is someone else's for the duration of the lease. Make certain, also, that your homeowners insurance covers a rental situation.

THE HOME SWAPPING NETWORK

If you won't be on the road constantly during your year off and trading down is distasteful to you, there are other possibilities. You can swap your house to cut your vacation costs elsewhere. You'll save on hotels, meals and maybe even a rental car.

There are exchange guides that list houses, condominiums, and townhouses that are available throughout the world. The two biggest are Vacation Exchange Club (800 638-3841) and Intervac (800 756-4663). For a modest fee, you can find a match in an area of the world that intrigues you. You then arrange a swapping of your houses for a particular period of time.

Generally, your homeowners insurance will cover this situation, since you're not making money on the deal. Once again, check with your agent.

You can even exchange cars. Check with your insurance company to see if this presents any coverage problems. Otherwise, you may be stuck with a rental car which is a major expense, especially overseas.

Writer, Geri Anderson of Oak Creek, Colorado, offers

some great advice on this subject. She traded the Florida condo she owns for a house in Wales. For two weeks, she lived in a 16th century bakehouse in Wales. She shopped frugally and cooked her own meals.

The idea of swapping or renting your house may scare you if you have many valuable items there. Anderson suggests closing off one room or having a locked closet for valuable items.

Another possibility is to keep jewelry and personal items in a safety deposit box. Another option is to have a relative hold onto valuable items during your time away from home.

Many people won't be comfortable with renting or swapping their house. They fear that their priceless possessions will be broken or that someone won't treat their house with as much care as they would. Although this is unlikely and there are safeguards against this occurrence, there is always the possibility that someone will trash your house.

But if you're just being obsessive compulsive about your "things," lighten up. If you can't, however, renting your house or swapping homes is not a viable alternative. You'll have to look at the other methods for financing time off.

SUMMARY

Michael Bamberger, a reporter for the *Philadelphia Inquirer*, found the right ticket for taking time off and traveling. In February 1991, he took a sabbatical from his job to work as a caddie on the European golf tour. His wife quit a good job with a New York advertising agency to come with him. Of course, he had a tidy book advance to help him cope with the expense of traveling.

You might not be as fortunate. Perhaps, you're hoping to find a job in a resort area as part of your travel plans. Ideally, you'll make a few bucks at the job and live cheaply in staff housing, if it's available. Once again, don't forget that even though the dream job doesn't live up to your expectations, your house back home might be committed to someone else.

Although there should be room in your year off budget for travel, make sure you're prepared to make sacrifices. There won't be any respites at airline clubs, unless you have some time left on your membership. You won't be upgrading to first class, unless you've stockpiled your coupons.

If you're used to taking spa vacations or staying at five star hotels, the travel experience during your year off may be disappointing. But if you're ready to thoroughly enjoy a year long travel adventure without worrying about what's piling up on your desk at work, we'll leave the light on for you.

HEALTH INSURANCE AND OTHER POLICIES

You're all suited up for an afternoon of snorkeling. You adjust your goggles and your snorkel, almost as if you know what you're doing. Start small, you tell yourself. You pick the snorkeling trail that's close to shore.

Sure, it's a little rough you notice as you're walking out toward the coral reef. Because you didn't invest in fins, you notice the rocks underneath your feet. Or at least you hope it's just a rock.

Despite these problems, you didn't take a year off, just to sit on the beach on a day like this. When the water is up to your waist, you put your face below the surface to look for fish. Quickly, you notice that your air-tight mask is filled with water up to your eyeballs. You stand up in the shallow water to drain your mask.

At that moment, you are hit by one of the waves. You fall and smash your fingers against the sharp coral. Well, enough snorkeling for today, you think while watching the blood gush from your knuckles. You remember the basic rule of first aid which is to run to the lifeguard and hold out your hand. She pulls out some bandages from her kit and gives you a look that says you're the biggest baby in the world.

The bandages do the trick, even though they look like they've been used before. Later, you notice a bigger problem. Your wedding ring won't come off. Days later, your knuckles are still swollen and painful, which prompts a visit to the doctor. Fortunately, however, there's no surgery or hospitalization required.

It's not just snorkeling that can do you in. Any of us non-athletes can turn a simple sport into a health problem, if we work at it. If you're at the beach, you can nearly kill yourself water skiing, surfing, jet skiing, sailing, or while participating in a dozen other activities. Actor Leonard Stabb, of *The Guiding Light*, was seriously injured in a hang-gliding accident.

Your hobbies might lead to accidents too. You might be injured playing tennis or while golfing. Even if you know what you're doing, there's always a danger of hurting yourself while using power tools in your home workshop or by burning yourself with a soldering iron while making a stain glass lamp.

Hopefully, your money-saving efforts won't lead to medical problems. If you're up on the ladder painting or working in the yard, you may make a stupid mistake that will be injurious to your health.

Even if you spend your year off doing nothing, there's a risk of spending part of it in the hospital. And it's quite clear that medical treatment of any kind will cost far more than the $25 charge to get your ring enlarged to fit over your swollen knuckles. Accordingly, your year off plan must take health insurance into account. It's not something you can cut out of your already-tight budget.

COBRA

Many experts estimate that your benefits package at work adds at least a third to your salary. It's a major part of your compensation package. Consequently, as you move toward taking time off, you must give every consideration to these benefits.

As we discussed in Chapter 9, when you negotiate with your employer for time off, money and job security aren't the only issues. Keeping your benefits during the year off is another important perk to win. And health insurance is probably the most valuable benefit your employer offers.

Ideally, you'll be guaranteed a job to return to after your time off. Hopefully, too, your employer will keep your health insurance in force for you during the sabbatical. If you've decided that time off is worth quitting for, you face uncertainty career-wise and insurance-wise. As things stand now, however, COBRA is one option for many readers.

No, COBRA isn't a creature you'll run into at *Jurassic Park*. It's a federal law that lets you buy insurance more reasonably from a former employer, as long as you meet certain conditions. COBRA is short for Consolidated Omnibus Budget Reconciliation Act.

COBRA doesn't apply to every employee who leaves the company. Among other conditions, the company you worked for must have twenty or more employees. Furthermore, there are certain qualifying events that trigger COBRA eligibility. Leaving voluntarily is a qualifying event.

Unfortunately, you don't get insurance for free with

COBRA. You're entitled to purchase health insurance at the employer's presumably low group rate, plus an administrative charge of two percent. That could still be quite steep, so it must be factored into your budget for the year off. But, by keeping your current policy in force, you shouldn't run into preexisting medical condition problems as you might with a new policy.

If you're able to use your company's downsizing plans to your advantage, you may have other insurance options. A more economical medical plan than COBRA might be offered as part of the separation package.

When you don't qualify for COBRA, look into coverage through your local Blue Cross/Blue Shield. They often offer no-frills coverage at a reasonable price. You might even pay less than the COBRA rate, although the coverage will be more restrictive. Your employer's health insurance policy will normally offer much more in the way of coverage, but those may be benefits you'll never use.

While you're shopping around for health insurance, don't forget to price a policy with any professional, social or fraternal organization of which you're a member. They may offer a low-cost group health insurance policy to members.

If you're a lawyer, you probably belong to a bar association of some kind. Even if you're a bartender in Malibu during your year off, you can still belong to that organization and purchase health insurance through it.

If you decide to open up a business during your time off, you might join the local Chamber of Commerce. That organization may offer a group plan to its members.

Consider joining an HMO, if you're family goes to the doctor a lot. Although the enrollment costs may be higher, your out-of-pocket expenses may be lower. Keep in mind that with an HMO, however, you sometimes are limited in your choice of medical providers.

You need a comprehensive health insurance policy that covers you and your family for any accident or illness. Don't make the mistake of buying a mail-order policy that only covers one dread disease. Stay away from group accident and hospital indemnity plans. They'll be practically worthless, if you run into medical problems.

HEALTH INSURANCE: DON'T LEAVE HOME WITHOUT IT

Even when you have a good health insurance policy, there are other issues to consider. In the last two chapters, we've given advice to readers who want to travel during their year off. Whether you leave the country or just the county in which you live, make certain your health insurance covers you while you're away.

Many HMOs and managed care programs have significant restrictions on medical treatment while away from home. Before you leave, contact your health insurance provider to see how emergency treatment is handled.

Obtain the list of preferred providers in the areas where you'll be traveling or living. Often, medical plans reimburse you at a lower percentage for treatment by a doctor who doesn't participate in your health insurance provider's program.

If you leave the country, your policy may not cover

you. In that case, you must purchase medical coverage in a travel insurance policy or an international medical plan. Make certain you've budgeted for this expense, since going without health insurance is no way to save money.

In addition to insurance, use a little common sense before leaving the country. Get a dental check-up so you won't run into problems. Make sure you have all the right shots for the area in which you're traveling. Take any prescriptions or over-the-counter remedies you'll need overseas.

While you're away, avoid eating or drinking anything that's going to cause you problems. And if you really want some medical problems to worry about, read Paul Theroux's article in the July, 1993 issue of *Conde Nast Traveler*. In vivid detail, he describes illnesses he's caught while traveling over the years. The article is appropriately entitled, *Parasites I Have Known*.

INSURANCE ISSUES

If you dream of doing wild and crazy things, your year off is not the time to do them. An accountant who went sky diving on her vacation found that out.

The twenty-four year old woman, after a day of training, jumped out of the plane at 2800 feet. Her main chute became tangled and didn't open. At 1800 feet, she managed to open the emergency chute which is difficult to steer. The accountant narrowly avoided power lines and bounced off several trees. Amazingly, her only injury was a sprained ankle.

The woman offered this tip: If you're going to sky dive, do it on the last day of your vacation, she advised from her hospital bed. But vacation time isn't the only benefit tied to your employer. If you're like most people, your insurance is tied too closely to your job. And health insurance isn't the only policy that you rely on your employer to buy for you.

In some families, the only life insurance is the group policy provided by the employer. You have all the insurance you need, as long as you work with that employer forever. Regardless of whether you take a year off, it's time to realize that you can't just rely on the insurance you get through work.

Although most employees get considerable life insurance through work, a separate policy is often necessary. Consider buying an annual renewable term policy which gives you the most bang for your insurance buck. You can't be turned down when the policy comes up for renewal. If and when you do leave your job, you'll still have the insurance you need. At worst, consider converting your life insurance policy from work, but remember it may be quite expensive.

Disability insurance is often tied to your job too. In too many instances, the amount you're paid depends upon how long you've worked for a company. You're not covered for a lengthy disability.

Consider an individual disability policy, especially if you'll be at a new job after your year off. You can save money by buying a policy with a ninety day or longer elimination period. The elimination period is a lot like the deductible. Your benefits won't begin until ninety days after you become disabled, but you'll be protected for the long term.

If you can't swing an individual policy, consider a long-term disability policy through a group association to which you belong. It won't cover you as thoroughly against disability but you'll at least have protection that is independent of your company benefits.

Although your auto policy isn't tied to your employer, unless you work for an insurance company or drive a company car, it's worth looking at when you're ready for a year off. As we mentioned earlier, your auto insurance premiums should drop if you're not running back and forth to work each day.

You should also cut your premium wherever possible, in order to keep your expenses low during your time off. Raise your deductibles, wherever possible. Follow crash dummies, Vince and Larry's advice, and drive carefully during your year off. Aside from the insurance issues, you can't afford a ticket during your time off.

SUMMARY

Although you may not get a paycheck during your year off, you can still negotiate for those other perks that mean so much. Perhaps, your employer will let you keep your health, life and disability insurance policies. Otherwise, you'll have to look elsewhere for coverage.

If you're forced to look elsewhere for insurance, it's another financial hurdle to overcome. But don't despair. Even as we speak, Hillary is working on health insurance reform. Until then, however, health insurance is a problem for you to deal with in planning your year off.

To keep your health insurance and other benefits, you may be forced to stay at work instead of taking a year off.

Perhaps, if health insurance reform becomes a reality, workers will not feel tied to a job they hate. If not at the national level, your state may implement legislation that will make health insurance affordable. Although health insurance is likely to remain expensive, there is a bright side. Hopefully, you won't have to cope with much stress during your year off. If you keep working at that same job without a break, it's a good bet you'll need that policy you get through work.

A survey from Northwest National Life in Minneapolis, Minnesota, tells us something we knew already. Stress in the work place can cause medical problems. The survey reports that seven out of ten workers said stress caused them frequent health problems.

There was another interesting finding. Thirty-four percent of the workers responding have given serious thought to quitting their jobs because of stress in the work place. Taking a year off need not have the finality of quitting and can help lead to a healthier life-style.

To a large extent, you can control your health during the time away from work. If you always complain that you're too busy to get in shape, you've run out of excuses. You'll have time to exercise and eat sensibly. You won't be tempted by power lunches or business dinners on the expense account.

Although your health should improve while you're off, take one more precaution. Before you approach your employer, get a complete physical to make sure all the body parts are working properly. Being sick is no way to spend your year off.

TIMING YOUR YEAR OFF

It's an annual ritual for you every December. You hit the stationery store to buy a personal organizer and calendars. You hand over your credit card for a Filofax, Day Runner, Scully or one of many other brands. After all, it's the only way to keep track of your crowded schedule for the next year. And being organized isn't inexpensive. The planners can cost $200, especially if you opt for the leather cover with your name embossed on it.

You're all set for the new year. Another year of meetings, last-minute flights to customers, twelve-hour days, heated confrontations with co-workers, and dragging yourself to work with the flu. Another year of trying to manage the precious little time you have, while spending little or no time doing the things you enjoy.

If it's not too late, save the money you'd spend on a calendar planner and organizer. If it's already bought, use it to work with some of the timing issues that can help you effectively plan your year off. With proper planning, a year off can help your financial situation so as to negate the adverse impact of losing a paycheck. Since the top Federal income tax bracket on earned income is 39.6 percent, there's a great deal of money at stake.

Once again, if you're getting your full salary during

the year off, these timing issues won't be important to you. But, if your paycheck is going to shrink or stop entirely, you'll need to pay particular attention to the tax issues affecting your time off.

NO TIME OFF FROM PAYING TAXES

In some ways, it has the makings of a good news/bad news joke. The bad news is that you won't have any money coming in during your year off. The good news is that you're going to be in one hell of a tax bracket.

Taking a year off, depending upon how you time it, can improve your tax bracket over one year or two. If you leave mid-year, your bracket will be lower for two years, not just one. The time off may cut the taxes you owe on the money made before you leave and after you come back.

If your tax bracket will only be low for one year, push as much income as you can into it. Accelerate your deductions into the tax year before you leave, so you can maximize their value. For example, double up on your charitable donations during the year when your tax bracket is high. The donation will save you more taxes than it will during your time off.

We talked in Chapter 4 about going through the attic to look for collectibles to help finance your time off. If you find any other useable property in good condition, donate it during your peak income tax year. Charitable gifts of property are deductible, subject to certain limitations.

If you're self-employed, defer income wherever possible into the year when you're taking time off. Hold off on sending bills until the end of your peak earning year, so you won't collect income until later.

Suppose you have a side business that you'd like to work on during your time off. The IRS may view that business as a hobby, unless you show a profit in three out of five years. Ideally, your business won't begin to make a profit until your time off. At that point, you'll probably be in greater need of the money and your tax bracket will be lower.

When you have a side business, you can control your income to some extent. If you're going to need a computer, fax machine, photocopier or other business equipment, you can usually write the entire purchase off on your Schedule C. By timing these purchases of equipment that you'll need eventually, you can curtail your income during the year while you're still working at your regular job.

Wherever possible, defer earnings on savings certificates into that year when your tax percentage will be lower. You can buy a certificate at your bank that pays the interest at maturity, not monthly. Although you're not compounding your earnings by reinvesting them monthly, you'll more than make up for it with the tax savings.

We mentioned before that this may be the perfect time to cash those savings bonds that have been gathering dust. Most people pay taxes on their savings bond interest when they cash them, instead of declaring the interest yearly. Although it was great to defer the taxes from year to year, it can mean a heck of a tax bill when they're cashed. If you're using savings bonds meeting this description to pay for your year off, you can minimize your tax obligation with the right timing.

When you do cash these bonds, the proceeds should

go immediately into your year-off account. Even though you're in a lower tax bracket during your year off, don't forget to pay estimated taxes on the interest from the bonds. Otherwise, you'll be hit with a penalty by the IRS at the end of the year for underpaying your taxes.

Recently, many personal finance experts have begun recommending savings bonds as a short-term investment vehicle. Although the interest rate isn't great, the tax advantages and safety are comforting. If your year off is at least six months away, you can buy savings bonds with the intent of cashing them when your tax bracket is lower. Remember, however, that savings bonds must be held at least six months before they're cashed.

Even if you're not using savings bonds to fund your year off, you can help your situation with the right timing of a year off. Bonds bought after January 1, 1990 and used for a child's education are tax free, if your income is below a prescribed amount. If you cash those bonds during your year off, you'll be redeeming them at exactly the right time.

Pay attention too to the date on which interest on bonds is paid by the government. Don't redeem them until after the semiannual interest accrual. With new EE bonds, the redemption value increases each month. After thirty months, however, the redemption value only increases twice per year. At that point, interest is paid on the anniversary of when the bond was issued and six months later.

Once you've chosen the month in which to redeem your bonds, cash them in on the first day. You get no extra interest by waiting until later in the month.

TAKING STOCK OF STOCK

As we've discussed before, you may be using your stock portfolio to partially fund your time off. Depending on your particular situation, you may face some unique timing issues.

As we discussed in Chapter 4, not every asset will be in your year off account prior to taking time off. If you have stock that can't be sold until your year off because you'll be faced with a large tax bill, you're in a dicey situation.

Stock is trickier to sell than savings bonds, because you're trying to get the best price for your shares. If you wait to sell for tax reasons, the price per share may be down. Similarly, you may be in a position where you're selling stock that's expected to increase in value, simply because it's the right time for tax purposes. Worse yet, you may be selling simply because you need the money.

Although 28 percent is the top tax rate for long-term capital gains, you may find yourself in a lower bracket during your year off. Conceivably, you'll be in the 15 percent tax bracket. As a result, you may be hesitant to liquidate those shares until then. Unfortunately, the shares may drop between now and then.

If most of the money for your year off comes from sources other than stock, you'll have a great deal of flexibility. If the time to sell isn't right, you can use other funds first and wait for the price per share to rise.

On the other hand, if you're selling stock at a loss, do so during your peak income year. You can take up to $3,000 in investment losses to offset your earned income.

It may be best to do any juggling of your portfolio,

before taking time off. Maybe you can sell those shares that are going in the year off account and use the capital losses to offset the gains.

Taking time off may have an impact on your other investments. For example, tax free municipal bonds may not be appropriate, since you'll be in a lower bracket.

Have a long chat with your personal financial adviser or accountant and see what's best for you. Discuss your plans for time off and ask for suggestions. Don't dump any stock until you know more about its long-term prospects.

But don't wait too long. The stock market may not cooperate with your plans for taking a year off.

OTHER TAX CONSIDERATIONS

It's not just your tax bracket that must be taken into consideration. There are many tax angles to consider. If you customarily earn more than the limitation for Social Security deduction, you may want to keep the year off to one calendar year not two. This may work out to be better than spreading out your income over two years and never getting to the point where Social Security is not deducted. Remember in Chapter 3 that we discussed using this extra money in your paycheck to help fund your year off. If you go beyond the Social Security maximum, you'll have extra money in your paycheck for the last few months of the year.

The timing of your year off won't, however, have any impact on the Medicare tax. You'll pay that tax on all the income you earn. In 1993, the Medicare tax was not deducted after you earned $135,000.

It's not just Social Security taxes that are affected by the timing of your year off. Personal exemptions are phased out if you make too much. If your adjusted gross income is too high, your itemized deductions may also be reduced. With good planning, you can avoid these tax implications that are associated with making too much money.

With the right timing, you might be able to qualify for an IRA deduction. You can get a full IRA deduction of $2,000, if your adjusted gross income is $25,000 or less on an individual return or $40,000 on a joint return. With a year off that stretches from mid-year to mid-year, you might qualify for full IRA deductions in two years.

There are other deductions that you normally can't take, because your income is too high. Hopefully, you won't be able to take the deduction for medical and dental expenses. You can only deduct the amount of your medical and dental expenses that is greater than 7.5 percent of your adjusted gross income.

The threshold for deducting miscellaneous expenses might be reachable during your year off. You can deduct certain miscellaneous expenses, if they exceed two percent of your adjusted gross income. Therefore, if you incur job-hunting expenses above that amount, you may qualify for a deduction. Remember, however, that you must be looking for a new job in your present occupation. Many readers who take time off will be looking for new careers altogether. Therefore, they won't be entitled to a deduction.

In Chapter 14, we'll talk about the impact of time off on other members of your household. We'll discuss how tough it is to swing time off, if you have children approaching college age. On the bright side, your income might be at a low point when it's time for them to apply for financial aid.

Finally, if you're adversely affected by President Clinton's new tax law, a big smile may come to your face. Because of your time off, you may avoid a tax increase.

OTHER TIMING ISSUES

Timing is a lot more than just taxes. With the right timing, you can keep your costs down as we discussed in Chapter 3. With a little flexibility, timing your purchases can save you money.

Let's look at an absurdly simple story problem that won't appear on the Scholastic Aptitude Test. A pizza parlor offers a large plain pizza for $5.99 on weekends. On Sunday through Thursday, that same pizza is $3.99. When's the best time to buy pizza?

Well, if you're saving for a year off, a good pizza night would be Sunday through Thursday. Some readers, however, won't be able to shift their paradigm. Pizza night is always Saturday night. Others will argue that two bucks doesn't mean anything in the grand scheme of things, so why change.

Two dollars may not make the difference in your taking time off, but your reaction says a lot about you. It means you're too rigid to take time off. Taking time off requires flexibility and a willingness to adjust your lifestyle. If you're inflexible, you probably will ignore these timing issues.

No matter how insignificant the savings, you should

be conscious of the impact of timing. At a gourmet cookie store, there's a last hour sale each day when the calorie-filled treats are half-off. A bakery has a similar sale every day before closing. If you don't want to give up cookies, you can have your cake and eat it too.

Some people would suggest buying day-old baked goods or baking your own. These are decisions for you to make. The only point is that rearranging your day results in savings that can be deposited in the year off fund.

To take a year off, you'll need to time your purchases, so you get the best price. You'll need to buy clothes when they're on sale, not at the last minute when you absolutely must have a new outfit.

According to one bank publication, you'll get a better deal on ski equipment in March. If you need a refrigerator, January and July are the best months to shop. The best deals on televisions come in May and June. During certain months, you'll be able to get the best price on furniture.

But even more importantly, if you're saving for a year off, take the time to shop around and make price comparisons before any purchase.

TIMING YOUR DEPARTURE

If you must sever your employment to take time off, you can still pick the best time to do it. Perhaps, you are nearing some pension milestone that's worth waiting for and delaying your time off. Obviously, if you're nearing the end of the year and can pick up a fresh batch of vacation by waiting until January to leave, it's worth postponing your year off.

Be wary, however. You can always find a good reason

to postpone your time off by waiting for some milestone, whether it's your annual raise or a work anniversary. If you're close to one of these dates, however, sit tight by all means.

By the same token, you certainly wouldn't want to lose money with bad timing. If your line of work gives annual bonuses in December, November would be a bad time to leave or bring up that you're interested in taking a year off.

Don't forget how important timing is when you approach your employer for time off. Remember the best time to negotiate is before your employer's busy season, not after when the company has all the time in the world to train someone else. Your leverage is greater, before the busy season even though you may not take the sabbatical until after it's over.

And for gosh sakes, don't go in after botching up a major project or losing an account. That's worse than bad timing.

SUMMARY

Because you'll have less money to work with during your year off, you'll need to make every dollar go farther. By paying close attention to timing, you can reduce your taxes and do more with your money.

Timing has always been important when it comes to investments. You don't want to be forced to sell an investment, just because you need the money for time off. There are many other considerations that go into that decision.

It's not just the problem of selling shares of stock or mutual funds in a down market. If you have holdings in silver or gold that you're using to defray the cost of a year off, you don't want to be forced to liquidate when the price is depressed.

Whether it's selling off your holdings or making purchases of any item, don't box yourself in a corner. You'll get the worst price when you are forced by time constraints to act in haste.

When speaking of timing, there's one more unavoidable issue. Maybe, you're starting to feel like the "Middle-Age Man" character on *Saturday Night Live*. The character would show up in people's houses to share the knowledge that only comes with age. He would always admonish the people he visited with this remark: "Quit looking at my gut. I'm working on it."

Whether you're a middle-age man or woman, whether you have a little bit of a gut or a washboard stomach, time is creeping up on all of us. It's time to consider taking time for yourself.

FAMILY TIES

It's just a pleasant little chat with the family around the dinner table. It's paper plates and pizza all around, the second time this week that Domino's did the cooking. Mom, Dad and the kids gulp down dinner, knowing that everyone has activities in about twenty minutes.

"Did I mention, honey, that I want to quit my job and take a year off?" one spouse says to the other.

"And I want to sail the Caribbean in my yacht," the other spouse replies.

"I'm serious. We'll cut back on our spending and live on one income ...yours."

"Gee, that sounds fair."

No matter who you live with, whether it's a significant other, spouse or whomever, it's not fair for just one of you to enjoy a year off. Your partner will be continuing to work ungodly hours and will feel even more pressure to earn a living. Ideally, you and your partner can take a year off together. But if only one partner wants a year off, it may make it easier for the other to take time off.

Taking a year off from work is a challenge, no matter what your family situation is. Initially, we'll focus on households where both adults work. For at least a year, these families must shift from two incomes to one. Let's start by looking at whether you can swing it. As a jumping off point, calculate how much you'll lose. Look at your take home pay and subtract the expenses you incur by working. Obviously, you'll spend less on commuting costs, clothes, lunches, and other expenses.

Don't inflate your spending estimates to achieve the result you want. It's easy to say you'll save thousands of dollars on your work wardrobe, but be realistic.

Don't forget about the indirect expenses that come from working. Perhaps, you eat out more than you'd like or serve more convenience foods at home than you would otherwise. Maybe, you pay for certain household expenses like cleaning help or grass cutting that wouldn't be necessary, if you had more time.

Depending upon how you plan on spending your time off, you may save on child care expenses. This may take an even bigger chunk of your paycheck than federal, state, local and Social Security taxes. Even with the child care credit you get on your income tax return, you may still save thousands of dollars.

On the other hand, you'll lose benefits and won't be making contributions to retirement savings plans. Your pension may suffer. You face the same issues we've brought up before, such as whether you'll do long-term damage to your career.

In many families, the second income pays for luxury items that couldn't be afforded otherwise. It might pay for a great family vacation or a child's summer camp. Maybe it pays for that restored 1966 Mustang convertible that you cherish or for remodeling projects.

In many instances, however, the second income is needed just to keep abreast of high mortgage payments or steep tuition bills. The second income keeps the family's head above water and is an absolute necessity. You may be approaching that period in life where your expenditures are ramping up not down, which makes taking a year off extremely difficult.

Most households are better off when both adults work, if you only look at income versus outgo. Once the expenses you incur by working are factored in, however, the economic benefit may be nominal. And to reap that economic benefit, you pay a price. You come home from work aggravated and spend less time with your family.

On the other hand, working provides non-economic benefits too. For some, a job provides self-esteem and social contacts. Your career might be extremely gratifying and spiritually rewarding.

Nonetheless, no matter how rewarding it is emotionally and financially, your job undoubtedly consumes too much of your time. In the end, deciding whether to take a year off is a life-style decision that you must make after examining all of these issues.

HONEY, I SHRUNK THE BUDGET

Whether only one or both adults earn a paycheck, it's time to reevaluate your financial situation. If it takes every penny of two incomes to keep up with your life-style, neither one of you is going to take time off. But even if you've come to believe that taking time off isn't right for you, you're still in for trouble if one partner loses his or her job.

No matter what your situation is, try out the one paycheck test. Pick one and live on it. If you can, live on the smaller one but at least try. If only one partner is taking a year off, immediately begin banking that person's check.

There are some obvious flaws with this approach. You're trying to bank one paycheck, but you'll still be incurring the expenses associated with working. On the other hand, once you get used to living on less, your situation will only get better when these expenses are curtailed.

As we've stressed so often, don't commingle the money you're saving with your other funds. Put it in the year-off fund right away. Except for credit-card debt and other high interest obligations, you shouldn't be paying off your loans with the money. Until you've cleaned up your credit card problems, you shouldn't even be thinking about taking a year off.

A low interest mortgage, however, is a totally different situation. For example, if you pay off a portion of your mortgage, you'll be helping yourself in the long term but it's not going to reduce your monthly obligation during the time off. Getting rid of your mortgage would be a more effective strategy, if you're hoping to retire in five or ten years. To take a year off, you need cash and lots of it.

And you'll accumulate that cash by banking one of your two paychecks. Perhaps, it's time too for your children, if they're old enough, to pitch in. No, they're not going to help fund the year-off account, but they may be able to help pay some of their own expenses. If they get a part-time job, it can reduce the amount you'll have to shell out on their behalf.

Every member of the family will have to make sacrifices for either one or both of you to take time off. It's going to be hard on everyone, but there will be advantages. You'll give up an expensive two-week family vacation, but in its place will be state parks, museums, ball games, hiking, biking, and playing together. Time off can mean you'll be on time for dinner with your family.

FROM DINKS TO DUNKS

There is no question that having children makes it much more difficult to take time off. Unless your child pulls down Macaulay Culkin's salary per picture, parents will have a tougher time financing time off than DINKS, double income, no kids or even SINKS, single income no kids.

For those readers who love acronyms, here's another possibility. You can go from being DINKS to DUNKS. During your year off, the two of you can become DUNKS, double unemployed, no kids.

If you think that's tough, pity the parents who want time off. They face a host of logistical and financial problems. For example, if they hope to travel during their year off, there's an immediate problem. The kids will need to stay put because of school or switch to a school district where you'll be located.

The problems of switching children from one school district to another may come into play, if you're financing your year off by trading down home-wise. Your permanent dwelling may be in a better school district than where you're renting. One possibility is for your children to remain with friends or relatives in the school district for the year.

Even if your children are older, there are problems. If

they're approaching college age, you have hefty tuition bills that you're facing. Of course, maybe there will be more financial aid in their future, if they apply after you've taken time off.

You might have some difficult decisions to make. Taking time off may mean that your kids will have to go to a good public college as opposed to a more expensive private school. It may mean that they'll need to take out more loans to finance their education. Aside from college, you may have other financial obligations, such as a wedding to pay for, that can cut into your funds for the year off.

Just as most families sit down to plan a vacation, taking a year off requires input from every family member. Taking a year off is a family project that has an impact on everyone.

It's important that you sit down as a family to discuss the sacrifices that everyone must make. Each family member should suggest ways to cut the budget. Hopefully, everyone will be willing to pitch in so that you can take time off.

SUMMARY

It's time to seriously consider a year off, if you and your partner can't even find time to even discuss the concept. During the little time you have together, you compare calendars for the week. Your appointment books are filled with late meetings, power breakfasts, and business trips that cut into the little free time you have.

Because of your busy schedules, you probably have to schedule sex. Somehow, spontaneity and romance goes out the window after a twelve hour day and three hours of personal errands.

The first thing you need to do is schedule some time together to discuss the idea of taking a year off. On second thought, you might want to schedule sex first and then get together to talk about the year off. On a more positive note, you won't have to go through these scheduling gyrations during your time away from work.

Whether you both work or not, whether your partner intends to continue working or not, this is a team project in which you both must participate. In fact, if your children are old enough, you should bring them in on the pow-wow, since all family members will be affected by it and will be making sacrifices.

Although it's not an ideal solution, maybe the two of you should take turns taking a year off. Assuming both of you earn roughly the same amount and get health insurance through your employer, it may work out well. Once one of you has taken time off and is back at work, the other can follow the same steps leading to a sabbatical.

Rather than flipping a coin to see who goes first, decide who has the better shot at negotiating time off. Certainly, if one of you can get time off without quitting, it seems to make sense for him or her to go first. It also helps to look at whose work situation is more intolerable.

There are advantages and disadvantages to going either first or second. By going second, you'll get a clear indication of whether taking time off is right for you. On the other hand, if your partner has a problem reentering the work force, the year off you've planned could be delayed. Although taking a year off requires discipline and sacrifice, it will be worth the price. For a year, you won't have to shortchange your family on the most precious of commodities, time. For a year, you won't have to juggle work and family responsibilities.

POSTPARTUM DEPRESSION

The bumper sticker says that the worst day on the beach is better than the best day at work. Unfortunately, it doesn't seem that way today. You look out the window and it's pouring. It's raining too hard to even walk the beach.

The gloomy weather should put you in the mood to write a depressing poem or song. Why bother, you say to yourself. You've already sent off four to publishers and everything has been rejected. The form letter says it all: "We're sorry but the volume of our mail won't allow us to respond personally to your letter. While your work shows promise, we find it is unsuitable for our present needs."

Worse yet, the budget's looking more ominous than the weather. The money you allotted for the month won't stretch that far, even if you live on macaroni and cheese for the next week. If you were back at work, the weather would be just as bad or worse, but at least you'd be getting paid to stare out the window. You and your spouse wouldn't think twice about making reservations for dinner at your favorite restaurant.

Work's starting to look a little better than it once did. You'd be getting coffee and chatting about how bad HBO is. Today would be payday. Instead it's time to go to the bank and withdraw more from your year-off savings fund. You question whether it would have made more sense to pursue your dreams, with a steady paycheck coming in.

Even if it were possible to get your old job back, you cringe at the thought. It would be a tremendous blow to your pride. Before you left, your co-workers gave you a cake and made a big fuss. Many came up to you to say that they wished they had the guts to take a year off.

So far, the time away from work hasn't endeared you to your family. The two months you've been off haven't exactly been quality time, to say the least. They're complaining that you're no fun to be around. You must admit that the rejection letters throw you into a funk and make you crabby.

It may be wet outside but your creative juices seem to be drying up. You painted a seascape earlier in the week, but nothing's inspiring you today. Maybe a change in scenery would help but you blew the housing budget on this condo which is paid up for the next month. There's no money in the budget left for a mini-vacation.

You also feel guilty about the money you're spending on piano lessons. Playing the piano was one of the many activities you wanted to try during your year off. Money, however, may not be the entire reason you're thinking of putting the lessons on hold. You find you hate practicing the piano as much as you did when you were a child.

Telling you to cheer up isn't going to help. When you take a year off, there will be days like this. There are bad days, even in paradise. Even when it's sunny outside, there will be times when you'll be sorry you decided to take time off.

FIGHTING THE YEAR OFF BLAH'S

When you take a year off, you'll be making some irrevocable decisions. You may not have a job to come back to in a year. Your career may never be as good as it is now. Financially, you may never recover. If the year off isn't everything you hoped it would be, you're likely to become depressed.

Depending upon the route you chose to finance your year off, there may be no turning back. If you've rented your home for a year so you can travel or live elsewhere, you're committed to the life-style you've chosen for the duration of the lease.

A sure guarantee of POSTPARTUM depression is bad planning. That's why the dress rehearsal in Chapter 8 was so important. You need to test your plan to see if it has any flaws.

To avoid POSTPARTUM depression, it is important to hit the ground running. Even though a year off is a long break from work, it can pass too quickly. Don't waste weeks on activities that weren't part of your dream.

If your plan involves a new computer, make sure it's up and running when your time off begins. A sure-fire guarantee of frustration and depression is to spend your first month reading the operating manual as you try to set it up. Don't find yourself playing with an unfamiliar word processing package and losing large chunks of your work. Nevertheless, if learning more about computers is how you want to spend your time off, enjoy yourself.

Most readers, however, may react far more negatively to computer glitches during their year off. It will be a reminder of how easy it was at work to call someone to fix those computer problems.

Setbacks in your year-off activities will undoubtedly lead to depression. The activities that looked so good from afar may not be as much fun as you think. As we warned earlier, doing these things on a full-time basis may seem more like work than play.

Aside from lithium, there are ways to deal with POST-PARTUM depression after you leave work. The primary tool is to recognize that a certain amount of depression is inevitable. When it occurs, simply recognize that it's un-avoidable. Hopefully it will pass quickly.

After years of professional success, it may take a significant adjustment to enjoy your year off. You may not feel as productive as you once were. If you're a person used to doing dozens of things in a day, winding down to a more relaxed pace may make you feel dissatisfied.

One solution is to engage in your year-off activities before leaving work. You need to read as much about these activities as you possibly can, so that you're not expecting some fantasy existence. The more you know, the more realistic you'll become about the activities you'll engage in during your year off.

If you're a writer, you have to develop a tougher skin for those rejection letters that will invariably come in. In that way, you're less likely to become depressed when the year off doesn't meet your expectations. Join a writers group, and not just because of the networking opportuni-ties. You'll learn what it's like to write on a full time basis and you'll have people to commiserate with when things are going badly.

To avoid depression, you also need to be ready for financial setbacks. Your car may need a new set of brakes or the refrigerator may conk out. There should be a cushion in your budget for these aggravating but unavoidable problems. Expect the unexpected and you'll react less negatively when the car or an appliance breaks down.

Only a truly naive person would expect every day of a year off to be perfect. It's up to you to enjoy the activities you've chosen to spend your day.

SUMMARY

When you were working seventy hours a week, someone told you to get a life. And when you take a year off, you'll finally have one. Unfortunately, it's going to be a little rocky at times with highs and lows.

There are going to be days when you'll be a little cranky. It's unavoidable. Recognize that and don't read more into it than you should.

To avoid becoming miserable during your year off, don't be goal-oriented. The only real goal is to learn more about yourself. Making money as an artist, musician, painter or writer isn't the goal *per se*. It's finding out whether you truly want to be an artist, musician, painter or writer. Financial success in those areas may come a long way down the road.

Taking a year off is the time for taking a shot at realizing your dreams. And if your dreams are less satisfying than you expected, it's time for a set of new ones. Even if that's the only thing you learn from your year off, it will have been a success.

ALTERNATIVES TO TAKING A YEAR OFF

Well, here we are at the last chapter and you've decided that taking a year off from work isn't right for you. Perhaps, the risks were too great and the benefits too few. Maybe, you've decided you'd rather shoot for early retirement instead of a year off. And by making that choice, you think you're doomed to thousands of Monday mornings, over-the-hump days, and TGIF's.

With no year off in sight, your fear is that your life will begin to resemble Bill Murray's predicament in the movie, *Groundhog Day*. Every day he got up and relived the day before. And for most people who work at a job they don't like, that's a frightening thought.

Or maybe your frustration is epitomized by a conversation overheard at the swimming pool. The woman in her sixties was talking about her children. "Of course, they hate their jobs, but what are they going to do? Everybody hates their job. But there's nowhere for them to go."

Now there's a pleasant thought for a gorgeous Summer day. Unfortunately, many people share that sentiment. Even if there's some truth to that statement, there are alternatives and not just a year off.

OPTIONS FROM A TO Z

If you can't swing a year off now, there are plenty of other possibilities. Hopefully, you've at least gotten your finances in order and are on solid ground. Even if the prospects for a year off look bleak now, that doesn't mean you have to abandon the idea altogether.

If you haven't set up a separate year-off account already, do it anyway. Maybe circumstances will be right down the road and you can give it a shot. Or maybe you can tap that account and use some of the funds to subsidize one of the many alternatives to taking a year off.

Maybe, with a little belt-tightening, you can swing part-time work. It will certainly put a little more balance in your life and increase the amount of time you can spend with your family. There's even some talk of law firms and accounting firms considering part-time partners.

Part-time work isn't the only option. If you're a two-income household, maybe one spouse can drop out of the work force for the time being.

Once your finances are in order, job sharing might be a palatable alternative. Another possibility is restructuring your current position to accommodate the life-style you want. Instead of pleading for a year off, try for more flexible hours. Many companies have opted for a four-day work week. Those four days may still be miserable for you, but the long weekends will be heavenly.

As we discussed in Chapter 6, there may be benefits your company offers that you've overlooked. Some companies let employees buy more vacation time. Others offer a specified number of weeks per quarter that you can take without pay.

We talked in Chapter 9 that something less than a year off is better than nothing. Whether it's an extra few weeks or an extra three months, any amount of time off may be enough to recharge your batteries. Perhaps, you can use any vacation time you've accrued in combination with a short leave of absence to take a mini-sabbatical.

On August 5, 1993, the Family and Medical Leave Act became effective. Pursuant to that law, you can take up to twelve weeks of unpaid leave to care for a newborn child, an ill family member, or recover from illness. Naturally, there are many exceptions spelled out in the law. For example, your company has to have fifty or more employees located within a seventy-mile radius. And you must put in a minimum of 1250 hours per year. Chances are, you're putting in twice that amount or more, which is why you're reading this book.

Your company might have a more generous family leave program that gives a longer amount of time off. There might also be fewer restrictions to qualify for family leave. These programs are good for the company and good for you. Your employer can reduce costs and retain quality employees. Programs like these can build employee loyalty and avoid turnover. In fact, family leave programs can help attract qualified applicants.

Telecommuting might be an alternative. There are many benefits to your employer and you. It may not be a dream come true but you'll at least eliminate the stress from going back and forth to work.

Perhaps, you can use some of the extra money for job counselling or to help make the transition to a new career. You might be able to get additional training or tuition reimbursement through your current employer.

Maybe it's time for a job that's less stressful, even though it doesn't pay as much. It might be possible for you to come in off the road and travel less, which might alleviate some of the stress and pressure you feel.

Or maybe there's a career out there that will incorporate some of the activities you hoped to engage in during your year off. And if you do take a new job, negotiate up front for more time off or a break before you begin.

If the stress is getting to you, see if your company has an Employee Assistance Program or offers stress reduction classes. Otherwise, look for a support group or a government agency that can help. Schedule an appointment with your doctor. Work in the yard more, which was suggested by one expert as a way to reduce stress.

In a recent newspaper article, it was reported that more women are buying boats to escape the stress of the corporate world. While boats and other expensive toys may relieve stress for some, be careful that you don't sink your budget and drain your year-off fund.

Financial problems can cause even more stress than your job. Aside from the goal of taking time off, you should be working to get your financial affairs in order. Once your head is well above water, you'll feel a lot less stress.

The year-off fund might be the source of capital you can use to start your own business. Of course, if you hope to start your own business, be prepared to put in even more hours than you do now. And in many ways, it may be even more risky than taking a year off.

LIFE-STYLE ALTERNATIVES

Maybe, a totally different life-style is called for as an alternative to taking a year off. We've stated frequently that most readers won't want to sell their home to finance time off. Nonetheless, you may be living in a house that forces you to remain at that high-powered job you hate.

If your mortgage payment and other expenses take every cent of your paycheck, you might want to consider trading down to a smaller and less expensive home. Once again, there's a dichotomy. You live in a beautiful house, but can't enjoy it because you're always working.

A less expensive home might make it possible for you to change your life-style. If you're house poor and over-extended, you may be chained to your desk for years to come.

Unfortunately, trading down to a less expensive home isn't encouraged by the tax laws. Unless you qualify for the one-time capital gains exclusion, you might owe a hefty tax bill if your home has appreciated in value. To postpone payment of those taxes, you have to trade up, not down, to a more expensive house. And that's not going to lead to a more modest life-style.

Another possibility is that if you must work, you can work in the climate in which you want to be. Obviously, certain jobs won't be available in Vail, Carmel or Boca Raton, but some will be. And if your place of employment can't be a few steps from the beach or the slopes, you can at least be a short drive away.

The August, 1992 issue of the ABA *Journal* contained interviews with lawyers who practice in Steamboat Springs, Colorado, Key West, Florida, and St. Croix in the U.S.

Virgin Islands. The attorney in Key West hasn't been able to take his boat out for months, because he's so busy. Nevertheless, if you must continue to work, it might be a great deal more tolerable if you're near the recreational activities you love.

Other attorneys mentioned in that article, however, were able to arrange their day to make time for tennis, golf, biking, and skiing. No matter where you are, if you can't take a year off, you can still look for ways to find a balance in your life between work and play. You have more control over this situation than you think.

To achieve the life-style you want, you might need to do more than just trade down to a less expensive house. You might also need to trade Nordstrom's for J.C. Penney's and Saks for T.J. Maxx.

You might also need to trade in some of those Yuppie toys like the car phone. You don't need the monthly charges.

As you alter your life-style, you can trade eating out for eating in. Make eating out a special occasion, not a way of life.

To achieve financial security, you might think you're lowering your standard of living. As you gain more time to do what you want to do, however, you'll find your standard of living has never been higher. All you're doing is living within your means.

As you become more financially secure, you'll become more independent. As you move closer toward financial independence, you'll be able to structure your life in a way that meets more of your personal needs. Most of all, there is nothing that gives a greater sense of freedom than knowing you can afford to leave your job at any time, instead of being locked in.

Don't forget that once your year off is over, you're not locked in until it's time to retire. One couple bought a boat and sailed it until they ran out of money. They sold it and are saving to do it again. We met a couple at a restaurant in Lighthouse Point, Florida, who were working on their second sabbatical.

Who knows. Maybe, things will work out so nicely that you'll be able to extend your sabbatical for an extra few months or years. Even though your job is still available at the end of the year off, you may wind up never going back.

SUMMARY

Taking a year off requires flexibility that many readers don't have. You'll need to change the way you spend money. You'll need to change your routine. You'll need to change your life-style.

In a *New York Times* Magazine article, Steven Ross of Warner Brothers recalled the advice given to him by his father on his death bed. "There are those who work all day; those who dream all day and never do a thing, and those who spend an hour dreaming before going to work to fulfill those dreams." Ross' father advised him to go into the third category, because there's virtually no competition.

Whether you want a year off or just a life-style that's less stressful, you need to dream a little and work hard toward that goal. There's more to life than work. Work at finding it. The satisfaction you derive will be immeasurable.

Index

Bibliography

ADVENTURE CAREERS - Alex Hiam

BOARDROOM INCENTIVES - Fredrick R. Adler

CASHING IN ON THE AMERICAN DREAM: HOW TO RETIRE AT 35 - Paul Terhorst

CONDE NAST TRAVELER - Paul Theroux

FIDELITY INVESTMENTS - Peter Lynch and Morris Smith

50 FABULOUS PLACES TO RETIRE IN AMERICA - Lee and Saralee Rosenberg

JOBS IN PARADISE - Jeffrey Maltzman

LOVE & PROFIT - James Autry

THE 100 BEST COMPANIES TO WORK FOR IN AMERICA - Robert Levering and Milton Moskowitz

THE PHILADELPHIA INQUIRER

POPCORN REPORT - Faith Popcorn

THE WALL STREET JOURNAL